R.E.S.P.E.C.T.

How Nonprofits and Private Sector Companies Can Blend Principles and Profits

Maryann Fleming

ISBN: 978-1-6848-9360-7 (Paperback)
ISBN: 979-8-8858-9177-6 (E-Book)

Library of Congress Control Number:

Cover and interior design Andy Meaden meadencreative.com

Contact the author at: flemingmae24@gmail.com

First printing edition 2022.

CONTENTS

ACKNOWLEDGMENTS

As I wrote this book, I found myself very grateful to have a supportive community, including family, as I worked through a sometimes-challenging process. I owe a very special thank-you to the individuals who really made a difference in these pages.

First, I'd like to express gratitude to my amazing daughter, Naomi. She's been a consistent inspiration to me and this work. It is an ode to her resiliency, steadiness, sense of humor, and empowered spirit that raising her as a single parent worked as well as it did. It enabled me to channel this influence into the formation of a nonprofit that served families with dignity, trust, respect, and empowerment.

At the start of the book-writing process, I found Lisa Haneberg, a writing coach, through the Carnegie Literacy Center. I had no idea how to shape a nonfiction manuscript, let alone write it. She helped me, an inspiring author, become organized and deal with the nitty-gritty of putting my thoughts to paper. Without her assistance it is clear I wouldn't have gotten anywhere. I appreciate Lisa's skills, wisdom, and perseverance. My manuscript would not have been a coherent work without her.

The next individual that I owe heartfelt thanks to is my dear friend Janet McCandless. Without her tireless help in reading some of the rough drafts, I never would have found a way to keep writing. Janet was consistently reassuring and appreciated all I did to get the book to where it is today. Her unwavering belief in me and this writing was valued and appreciated.

There were also my wonderful friends Susan Patton Fox and Shelia Mahoney, who read an early draft. They were especially helpful since the version they read was awfully rough. I thought they were brave to wade through that copy and extremely kind with their feedback!

I discovered Katherine Tomlinson with Story Authority through a mutual author. She is a miracle worker when it comes to editing a book. Katherine served as an experienced and effective reviewer. She was able to steer me toward cleaning up and formatting the book in a way that makes sense to anyone who picks it up.

A special thanks goes to Kate Victory Hannisian. She is the owner of Blue Pencil Consulting and has many years of professional writing experience, helping others to compose books, articles, blogs, and you name it regarding writing. Among writers, Kate is a content editor extraordinaire that looked for grammar issues, spelling mistakes, word usage, overall consistency in the manuscript, and flagged spots where edits were needed for clarity's sake. And I hate to admit there were a few of those. Much gratitude to you, Kate, on helping me finish the book.

Andy Meaden of Meaden Creative has had over twenty-five years of experience in graphic design. I was so lucky to have him work on my cover and interior design. He is simply fabulous. We had several Zoom chats to determine what I wanted. I found Andy to be exceptionally competent, experienced, and lovely to work with. For example, he gave me at least ten potential cover designs to consider and then made changes on the sample I chose. I would not hesitate to work with Andy again.

And last but certainty not least, hats off to all of those who helped with the nonprofit business I ran for twenty-five years! Especially the contributors that include participants, educators, funders, volunteers, staff, board members, school and community partners, local hospitals, and government contributors.

These folks added their awesome energy in helping to make that charitable organization successful. Without their care, insights, hard work, funding, and partnerships, I wouldn't have had the opportunity to establish such a remarkable family center.

INTRODUCTION

How Nonprofits and the Private Sector Can Blend Principles AND Profits

"If you want happiness for an hour, take a nap. If you want happiness for a day, go fishing. If you want happiness for a year, inherit a fortune: if you want happiness for a lifetime, help somebody."

Chinese Proverb

The letters that make up the word RESPECT stand for notable concepts you will find throughout these pages. **R**esiliency, **E**mpowerment, **S**ocial justice, **P**articipant-driven services or products, **E**motional intelligence, **C**ompassion, and **T**rust are these values. I strengthened myself emotionally using a combination of these very concepts. These principles continue to serve me well on a professional and personal level. All business can thrive by practicing values.

Organizations can implement ideals by showing the world they are out to do good as well as make money. Businesses can often be rewarded by enhanced revenues. People will buy products, services, and goods they know to be sustainable, work for the environment, and add intrinsic value to the buyer, all the while making the consumer feel like they did a good thing.

The same goes for nonprofits. A prospective donor (whether it's a foundation or an individual) will gravitate to the nonprofit that is able to demonstrate that they enhance the community through their well-run organization and good work.

The first time my mom, a longtime educator, walked into the nonprofit family center I founded, her eyes glistened with tears. She squeezed my hand and whispered, "It's beautiful." That message went straight to my heart. It meant everything to have my mom's approval. She saw something that was significant for the community because it offered valuable services and a positive environment.

I have worked in the nonprofit business sector for thirty-five years. Over that time, I established a well-designed, well-run family center in an underserved neighborhood in the Bay Area of California. I accomplished this mission by intuitively applying the values inherent in RESPECT.

The principles that make up RESPECT represent the values (e.g., resiliency, empowerment, social justice, participant-driven services, emotional intelligence, compassion, and trust) that we need to be applying to every aspect of our society in order to advance. Creating community through cooperation with a goal of social justice and empowerment is just one of the pathways to transformation.

This book was designed for businesses of any size, including nonprofits and for-profit organizations. I discuss some of the differences between these two business models, which are substantial. However, there are plenty of ways these types of business have learned and can continue to learn from each other.

My perspective is from a nonprofit values position, borrowing solidly from successful for-profit business practices. When nonprofit concepts come up (e.g., participant-driven services, board of directors, or fundraising), please understand this essential information could also be applied toward a commercial enterprise.

You can choose to ignore these tried-and-true business strategies or decide to learn from them. The business world is interconnected.

Questioning everything is a *key* concept. It appears repeatedly in major components in this book. Develop the wise use of appropriate querying. Think of asking questions as an effective device that can allow you to dig deep and learn about your subject matter.

The necessary legal precautions require that the names of the center, the persons involved, the exact area, the school (e.g., Bay Elementary School North is a fictional name), neighborhood, and city where the people associated with it have been changed or not mentioned. However, the main takeaway is that each story included in this book is true and really happened.

RESPECT contains truly vital components for business of all kinds. These particular principles can be utilized to yield exponential success. Imagine an improved work environment, enhanced productivity, increased profits or funding, and an enlightened set of values. These values are so beneficial and could readily be applied to our personal lives as well. They can work to heal, restore, and repair our emotional bodies.

RESPECT and its concepts are crucial to apply regularly. I will make suggestions throughout these pages on how to implement these values. In these pages you will find information about how to strengthen your business by using excellent techniques that, in turn, can help you to turn a profit. Implementing and using values can also help for-profits because it can create a better workplace and help employees become more connected to the organization's goals.

I'm making recommendations from years of experience in business and dealing with hardships. These suggestions include things I wished I had done, mistakes that I made, and achievements that I attained.

Whenever I could, I matched what I understood from experience with pertinent information from books and online articles.

The terms "boards" and "board members" are used interchangeably throughout with "trustees." I do understand the difference between the definitions of the two. However, it became extremely redundant to keep saying "board member" over and over. So, I made a judgment call and inserted "trustee" in numerous places.

"Programs" and "services" are switched throughout, generally meaning the same idea. With business, I utilized a number of words to describe the entity, including enterprise, business sector, and company. In context, they mean approximately the same thing.

RESPECT is written mostly for managers, owners, board chairs, executive directors, or those who have decision-making responsibilities.

Let's take collective action. Our world is in crisis as witnessed by widespread social injustices and other unwieldly problems. It is time try on a new paradigm.

This is a book about a wonderful, exciting, and sometimes unbelievably stressful adventure of establishing and running a thriving business. I did it by seeing the nonprofit as a business and using the ideals that make up RESPECT.

How I came to start a nonprofit

January 7, 1975, still stands as one of the most important days of my life. I gave birth to a healthy seven-pound baby girl named Naomi, who was delivered at home. This special event happened in a tiny studio apartment in Michigan with a rural OB-GYN who was willing to come to people's homes.

As my baby came into the world, the doctor said, "It's a girl type." While thinking that was an odd statement, I fell in love with my daughter at first sight. I couldn't believe my good fortune.

I had Naomi at twenty-two, married her dad at twenty-three, and divorced at twenty-six after some rocky years and the inevitable conclusion that this wasn't working. Since I had three younger sisters that I had watched out for as I was growing up, I thought, how hard could it be, taking care of a child? I saw myself as capable.

Yet, the reality of being a young woman stigmatized by single parenthood in the mid-1970s, shy of a college degree and having a small child, turned out to be a formidable challenge.

My big "Oh my goodness, what have I done?" moment came just months after the divorce, when my ex moved to Seattle with his new family. I was now a single parent, and it was all up to me! Every. Single. Bit. Of. It.

I struggled financially for years and didn't receive any monetary support from my ex until my daughter was a teenager. Naomi and I moved to the Bay Area in 1984, when she was nine years old. I had been selling advertising for a local monthly publication, which I enjoyed, but it clearly didn't feel like my life's work. The time was ripe for a change to more meaningful employment on all levels.

I got a job five months after I moved, at a publication that wasn't nearly as good as the community monthly in Michigan. I was scared and penniless with a growing child. The periodical served a small, high-end market in the Bay Area.

While it was a tough job because the magazine was difficult to sell, hope was right around the corner. Soon after, I was invited by a nonprofit to help them do drug/alcohol prevention training at my daughter's school.

I had started volunteer teaching a month after we moved to the Bay Area. I enjoyed it. The work created an odd but hopeful balance with selling advertising for the less-than-stellar magazine. Fortunately, the nonprofit I was doing training for recognized I had the necessary skills and created a full-time position for me.

For ten years, I established and ran a parent component of a Drug Abuse Resistance Education (D.A.R.E.) organization. I was so relieved to finally have a job I could embrace wholeheartedly.

The D.A.R.E. program, founded in Los Angeles in 1982, came to San Francisco in the mid-1980s. At the time, it was a drug/ alcohol prevention program for children and teens taught by police departments across the country. This was a nonprofit program that reached popularity nationally when the Reagan administration's "War on Drugs" got going and the slogan "Just say no" was popularized.

The parent curriculum we developed was well researched and specialized in teaching parents and caregivers positive discipline, effective child-parent communication skills, building their child's self-esteem, and drug prevention strategies. It incorporated important concepts you will see in this book, including resiliency, social justice, trust, and empowerment.

I had an inside track to understanding the effectiveness of the parent curriculum I was developing. I participated in many professional trainings on how to be an effective parent/caregiver. My attendance at these programs ensured I was on the right track. However, what really helped guarantee excellence was that my daughter gave the best reviews I could imagine.

Not telling her in advance of my intended experimentation, I would go home from workshops and try out what I learned. Being a smart kid, she would say, "Is that a new technique you learned today, Mom? I like it. Keep using it." Or, "I'm not sure about that one."

The nonprofit organization I founded had to do with children and community. I knew from personal experience that people can use support in raising their children. Parenting can be one of the toughest jobs in the world to do effectively.

Child-rearing presents numerous challenges. These include finding the best affordable health care, the appropriate schools, affordable housing, and work that offers flexibility and enough money to support a child.

The primary key to creating the aid that allows a youngster, family, and community to thrive is empowerment. I took this concept under consideration when I created the nonprofit that I ran for twenty-five years.

One of the elementary schools I served in 1992 was in a neighborhood in the Bay Area that had more than its fair share of problems. Yet, it was a great school. The teaching staff was exceptional and offered parents numerous helpful social services free of charge.

This group of educators at what I am calling the Bay Elementary School North received a grant from the State of California's Department of Education called Healthy Start. That year, I was working closely with the staff to offer their families components from the parent curriculum I had developed. At the same time, I was invited to join their mandated Healthy Start advisory board.

The program's purpose was to provide comprehensive, school-community integrated services and activities to improve the lives of children, youth, and families. The services were catering to the issues of the parents and children. The grant award criteria required that 50 percent of the students were eligible for free and reduced meals in the lower grades.

As an advisory board for the school's grant agenda, our responsibilities included guiding the school's Healthy Start practitioners and services. We supported them in implementing the best practices in the educational and social work field. Halfway through the school year, it became clear that the neighborhood where the school was located needed more community leadership and support.

Local problems were adversely affecting the students' parents, including gang violence, lack of safety, income inequality, and lack of transportation. One of the advisory board members was working on her doctorate at UC Berkeley and had a grant to write. She found an excellent opportunity for money from the State of California, Office of Child Abuse Prevention (OCAP), for a Community Empowerment grant.

The funding application asked recipients to create a strong external environment because OCAP's research showed that healthy communities had fewer incidences of child abuse. We wrote the grant, and I added aspects of resiliency, social justice, trust, and empowerment.

Truly against all odds, ours was one of five projects selected by the state to create and build a healthy community. A month into the implementation planning, a group of parents, community members, and educators chose me to become the first executive director. I proudly accepted the challenge. This is where I learned and practiced the lessons and principles I share throughout this book.

Chapter 1: A GIVE-AND-TAKE EXCHANGE *Nonprofits; For-profits*

"A fundamental concern for others' lives ... would go a long way in making the world the better place we so passionately dream of."

Nelson Mandela

Nonprofit: *Charitable nonprofits embody the best of America. They provide a way for people to work together for the common good, transforming shared beliefs and hopes into action. They give shape to our boldest dreams, highest ideals, and noblest causes.*

What Is a Nonprofit, councilofnonprofits.org

For-profit: *Used to describe an organization or service that exists to make a profit.*

dictionarycambridge.org

It is necessary for a peaceful revolution to include work, which is often referred to as a four-letter word. Our global surroundings are going through a huge upheaval as evidenced by all the earthly problems. This list might include super-contagious disease, unethical politics, the harmful environment, offensive business practices, and serious divisiveness, to name just a handful.

It is due time to reinvent our world and our work life. However, there is hopeful news. There are several sectors of business, including nonprofits and for-profits, that are adopting concepts and principles from each other. We can start now and encourage this needed transformation.

Nonprofits evolved from the idea that they would no longer be just about making money. Charitable organizations want to make the planet a better, more caring place to live. Nonprofits place their values first and everything else should follow.

As mentioned, for-profits are about creating wealth, and some are extremely good at it. How then can the two business models help each other?

For starters, nonprofits must move to adapt more business practices while keeping their mission intact. Commercial enterprises need to exercise their values. Principles should be embedded in the infrastructure of each to support their organization and its growth. These fields can educate each other.

Business can be beneficial to humans

For-profit companies are primarily in the moneymaking business, but some are incorporating principles to the way they work. They are discovering that doing good can be excellent for business.

Simultaneously, nonprofits—which are legal corporations—are using for-profit business strategies with advantageous results. Nonprofits are working toward maturing as a sector.

Nonprofit

Serves the public and aims to cure society's ills and provide for its needs

Does not seek profits

Has no owners but has a board or directors that provides oversight

Does not pay taxes

Recycles profits back into the organization and its activities

Uses outreach and networking to engage participants and collaborators

Can have a Chief Executive Officer (CEO) or Executive Director (ED)

For-Profit Business (or Private Sector)

Has no legal duty of working for the welfare of others

Seeks profits

Has a board with possible shareholders

Pays taxes (or might be paying taxes)

Profits go to company's owners and/or shareholders

Uses marketing and advertising to attract customers

Has a CEO or owner that runs the show (or the equivalent of)

Charitable organizations are waking up to the need to see themselves as the business they are. They can no longer run randomly and expect great results. While strategic planning used to be the centerpiece and a necessity, it no longer carries the weight it once did. It has been replaced by more agile methods.

The tools mentioned herein that nonprofits might adapt from the for-profit arena include strategic thinking, selling (e.g., marketing, and fundraising strategies), sustainability, running the nonprofit like a business, and executive coaching.

Some of those in the for-profit sector are applying their ideals to a mission or values. Along with this, numerous moneymaking corporations are adopting a *social responsibility agenda* (SRA). An SRA is a business project that benefits a group of people or has the company provide positive alternatives to a social problem.

Multiple for-profits have a nonprofit division or reward their employees with a small financial donation given to a nonprofit for sitting on charitable boards, sponsoring philanthropic events, or volunteering to help in other ways.

Our business world is rapidly shifting. Let's take advantage of this time. The lines between best practices for nonprofits and for-profits can be reduced by realizing that there is much to be gained by using recognized business strategies, regardless of who initiated them.

Examples of For-profit Companies Taking on Noble Work

- *Patagonia:* Delivers outdoor apparel and is committed to protecting and preserving the environment.
- *Ikea:* Supplies affordable furniture and other decorative household items. Dedicated to improving the lives of children through their generous funds.
- *Newman's Own:* Gives us an array of top-quality groceries. Donates 100 percent of their profits to various charities.
- *Legos:* Toymaker offers projects aimed at making a better world for children that includes learning and educational opportunities.

- *Warby Parker Eyeglasses:* Through their Buy-a-Pair, Give-a-Pair, Warby Parker makes a donation to their nonprofit partners to bring prescription eyewear to developing countries. They have donated eight million eyeglasses since 2010.

These days, values are essential business tools. Nonprofit and for-profit companies must act upon their values.

According to Vivek Ramaswamy, author of *Woke, Inc.*, America's corporations have a way to go in this regard. He feels that, "Corporate America's social justice is a scam. The modern woke-industrial complex divides us as a people. By mixing morality with consumerism, America's elites prey on our innermost insecurities about who we really are. They sell us cheap social causes and skin-deep identities to satisfy our hunger for a cause and our search for meaning, at a moment when we as Americans lack both."

Ramaswamy should know. He ran tech companies and a large biopharmaceutical business. He does not mince words and I don't blame him. Let's get rid of the negative mix of superficial values and capitalism. It is time to put our money where our mouths are and make sure that our ideals are real, we stand by them, and they are deeply embedded in our work culture. This goes for nonprofits as well as for-profit entities.

According to a Gallup poll, just 27 percent of US employees believe in their company's values (see "Few Employees Believe in Their Companies' Values," by Nate Dvorak and Bailey Nelson on gallup.com).

Genuine company values should nurture teamwork, support knowledgeable decisionmaking, communicate the company's objectives, and help ensure hiring decisions are the right fit.

They can be the workhorses that we can apply to shore up establishments of all kinds. Values are a powerful influencer and can strengthen the business and enhance positive employee satisfaction.

Nonprofits can advance their systems by integrating more of the nuts and bolts of running a business. For-profit business should pay attention to the implementation of principles and absorption of them. There is much to benefit both types of organizations by using each other's strategies.

To get you thinking about what values can enhance your organization and make a profit, see the websites listed at the end of this chapter. Your business is unique. The ideals you decide on should be specific to your organization.

The human condition seems to dictate that we ignore our problems, not admit our mistakes, and manipulate or blame others. Unfortunately, this negative mindset is part of business.

The primary concepts in this book are meant as a balm with positive solutions to redeem and surpass our existing boundaries. They are intended to allow nonprofits and for-profit businesses to use techniques, regardless of their label, for growth and achievement.

For-profit business ideas to put into practice

- For-profits can adapt select principles in their work and live by them.
- Predatory capitalism is destined to go out of fashion. The new world ethics won't stand for it. Adopt an innovative approach to business that integrates values in the workplace and doesn't hurt profits.
- For-profits need to get in their heads that they can still make lots of money and have values they believe in and implement.

Nonprofit business opportunities

- Pay attention to sustainability (nonprofit or otherwise) practices that produce longevity.
- Run your nonprofit consciously as the business it is.
- Learn from profit enterprises what their best practices are. Select and modify them to fit your needs.

More research on values

- Core Values List, https://jamesclear.com/core-values
- "70+ Examples of Core Company Values and How They Shape Your Culture," David Darmanin, https://www.hotjar.com/blog/company-values/
- "The Importance of Establishing Company Core Values—and How to Define Them," Vivian Maza (March 26, 2019), forbes.com, https://www.forbes.com/sites/forbeshumanresourcescouncil/2019/03/26/the-importance-of-establishing-company-core-values-and-how-to-define-them/?sh=48831a1c49af
- "Life Reimagined: Mapping the Motivation That Matters for Today's Consumer," https://www.accenture.com/bg-en/insights/strategy/_acnmedia/Thought-Leadership-Assets/PDF-5/Accenture-Life-Reimagined-Full-Report.pdf
- "Few Employees Believe in Their Companies' Values," Nate Dvorak and Bailey Nelson, gallup.com

Books

- *You Don't Have to be Ruthless To Win: The Art of Badass Selfless Service*, Jonathan Keyser. Lioncrest Publishing (2019).
- *Woke, Inc.: Inside America's Social Justice Scam*, Vivek Ramaswamy. Center Street (2021).
- *Principles: Life and Work,* Ray Dalio. Simon & Schuster (2017).
- *Dare to Lead: Brave Work. Tough Conversations.* Whole Hearts, Brené Brown. Random House (2018).

Chapter 2: EMPOWERMENT MATTERS *Empowerment*

"Go to the people. Learn from them. Live with them. Start with what they know. Build with what they have... When the task is accomplished, the people will say we have done it ourselves."

Lao Tzu

Empowerment: *Authority or power is given to someone to do something. The process of becoming stronger and more confident, especially in controlling and claiming one's life.*

Oxford English Dictionary, online edition

Participant-Driven Services: There is no "official" definition of participant-driven services, so I define it as:

Stakeholders are asking for and involved in selecting services, programs, and/or goods that will benefit them and others.

Is my idealism showing—again?

When I was a child, my mother repeatedly called me an idealist and said my feet didn't touch the ground and my head was in the clouds. It seemed like it wasn't a particularly good thing. However, when I discovered the nonprofit business field, I couldn't believe my luck. I felt like I had uncovered a whole group of like-minded dreamers who wanted to put their principles into action.

Now, many years of experience later, I have become well informed and gained invaluable skills in business. However, with a few significant live-and-learn lessons under my belt, I realize how much professional insight and for-profit business ingredients are crucial for running a thriving enterprise. After all, nonprofits are a business.

I was drawn to nonprofits because they were so value driven. That spoke to the need for creating positive outcomes for social problems (hence the idea of R.E.S.P.E.C.T.).

Yet, while I worked in the nonprofit world, I found myself leaning into for-profit business practices that really worked. Wouldn't it be great to use best practices from both business fields to generate the longevity most organizations crave?

Is that what I said?

In the modest beginnings of the nonprofit I founded, while we were moving in, three elderly neighborhood women stuck their heads in the door. Over the commotion, one yelled to me, "What's going on here? What is this going to be?"

I shouted back, "A family center." They looked at each other. The spokesperson for the group said loudly to the other two, "Oh, it's going to be a sandwich center." Then they walked away before I could correct them. I had to smile. A sense of humor is a requirement in any type of work, as is empowerment.

Empowerment via participant-driven services

Empowerment and participant-driven services are values. How then could these principles generate a profit? Increased revenues can happen because people are seen not only as the stakeholder but an important part of the process. Regular folks want to be seen and heard. They want their opinion to matter. And if they feel they are helping to get the word out about your services or products, all the better.

There is little mystique to the idea that to harness collective power, you must figure out how to relate to the populations you are investing in. Additionally, you need to engage and establish ongoing connections. In other words, you must listen to the voice of potential program attendees and trust what they are talking about. This was my first task in 1993 when I oversaw the creation of a center to form a healthy community in which to raise children.

While this is a different approach that for-profit corporations don't avail themselves of, it is akin to market research. The question that's asked is something like, do they have a buying audience for their products or services?

Participant-driven services are longer in duration and can take a more personalized approach to determine services and create civic purpose. While this is a community-building nonprofit strategy, that doesn't mean that corporations don't have something to learn. The implementation of real values could help. Keep an open mind and find out what may function well for your company.

Participant-driven services

One of the ways to begin empowering people is through offering opportunities for them to request services, programs, or consumer goods. Offering participant-driven services is one of the most effective methods of encouraging individuals to cooperate with and support your ventures.

It ensures involvement in programs/services/merchandise down the line.

Getting your community engaged is essential no matter which stage you are in. For-profit business can see it as member or subject engagement. Focus groups and surveys are widely used in business to determine the audience for a product or service and how to proceed. This is a way for companies to begin to build the value of empowerment.

This book is not an exhaustive collection of ideas for participant engagement. However, it does offer a group of potential tools. These strategies are the foundation or the building blocks for offering these kinds of services or products. This collection of approaches, including community mapping, advisory boards, and a needs assessment, is instrumental.

For example, if you are looking for understanding on how to move forward, use an assessment or a survey. It can give accurate information on the programs, products, or services to offer. These excellent strategies make effective stand-alone(s) or can be used in tandem with other procedures.

While it is understood that the terminology for describing participant-driven services is "nonprofit speak," don't let it turn you off. Call it what you like, but know concepts like empowerment can drive the change we need. Creating a more nurturing environment requires a different mindset, in which all participants feel they matter and are "seen."

Participant-driven services and empowerment refer to meaningful business models based on listening to people and then doing something about an issue or interest accordingly. Participant-driven services create empowerment and vice versa. Participant-driven services and intentional empowerment strategies can then form community.

You want to empower potential participants by discussing their concerns and asking what they think the provider or business can do about it. Execute a thorough needs assessment/survey of the community to find out what the problems and concerns are.

Then see how services and programs or products can address these needs and concerns.

Participant-driven services have input from and can often be led by the community you are reaching out to. There are numerous strategies. They include community mapping (understanding strengths and limitations), advisory boards, and needs assessments (surveys). Participant-driven services are included in empowerment, since it is one of its expressions.

My initial participant-driven services

The first participant-driven resources I oversaw were culled directly from an extensive needs assessment. These included parent-child activities, safety workshops, English as a second language classes, an exercise program, and a nutrition series. These initial services lasted three years with strong attendance.

Several years passed before people started to ask me directly for what they truly needed and wanted as they gradually began to trust in the process of asking then receiving. This was a progression that didn't happen overnight.

Once people realized that we were willing to do as we said in offering services requested by our neighbors, slowly but surely, numerous individuals began to make what I felt were significant requests. These included an early childhood education service and an after-school program. Empowering people in the community with participant-driven services was working.

You have a short time frame from when you receive participant requests to when you need to start designing and offering these programs (three to six months at the most). I was fortunate to have a beneficial partnership with the local elementary school staff. The school's early childhood educators helped me develop an early education program in just three months. I still remember the small, yet remarkable yellow and orange plastic picnic table from a garage sale that became the first snack table.

The valued partnership with the Bay Elementary School North (N)

The Bay Elementary School N (this is a fictional name for the real school) community that we grew out of was a valued partner, as was their excellent staff. They entrusted me to oversee the project and all that meant. I was empowered by the staff to run the nonprofit as I saw fit.

All the while, I was working on creating *community* empowerment.

Never once did the educators say I was on the wrong track. They were very heartened by the strategies I was applying to the work. They gave me the thumbs-up over and over. They were true cheerleaders and rallied parents to participate in our services.

It honestly came in handy to have various supports from the Bay School, since there were many financial start-up challenges. We were given $100,000 each year for three years. To give you a sense of the fiscal trials we faced, our annual rent for 4,500 square feet was more than $50,000 a year, and my first-year salary was $30,000. Doing the math shows there was only $20,000 left for services.

Thankfully, the school chipped in what it could from its unrestricted funds to help participant-driven services get the footing they deserved.

When I think back, realistically, we had less than a 50/50 chance of making it. After the grant period ended, the representative of the state grantor office confided in me that she hoped at least one of the five grantees made it past the three-year annual grant period.

We were the only recipients of those dollars that went on to establish longevity. Hindsight being 20/20, without the help of our partner school, Bay Elementary N, we probably wouldn't have made it.

The staff at our partnership school helped support initial efforts at the nonprofit in many ways:

- They secured a lawyer from the local office of a large international law firm to help us obtain our IRS 501(c)(3) status and State of California franchise tax board paperwork.
- The teachers created our first early childhood education service and the after-school program requested by the community.
- The school gave us some of its unrestricted grant money to use toward the renovations we needed to do for our programs.
- They introduced us to supervisors who supported the center in obtaining government funding.
- They procured funding for us from local foundations.
- They served as our first board of directors.

- They were the best group of supporters you could imagine. What I learned by implementing a conscious empowerment process for the neighborhood is to have patience. I am impatient by nature, yet it's imperative to let this process unfold as naturally as possible. And I am so glad I did, because the benefits were immeasurable.

The school assisted us repeatedly, since they believed in the work we were doing. And so did people in the community. It feels gratifying to hear neighbors' needs and to respond appropriately. You can create the programming folks have asked for, ultimately making a better, safer, and more empowered community.

Think about participant-driven services

1. How might you apply participant-driven services to your work?
2. How are empowerment and participant-driven services related?
3. What method could you use to obtain feedback from the people you want to reach?
4. What are a few ways that most companies could benefit from participant-driven services?
5. Why is it essential to empower people, and how can you do it by offering the products or services you do?

For-profit ideas to put participant-driven services into practice

- Participant-driven services is a concept that can translate into market research. The idea is that you gather people to value their opinions on your products or services.
- Participant-driven techniques (or a variation thereof) can help produce trust in the business field.

- Use the concept of empowerment and all its values to integrate these principles into the company.

Nonprofit participant-driven service opportunities

- Ask people what they need and then give it back to them in the form of programs and services. It is empowerment at its best.
- Participant-driven services (in all forms) develops the individuals participating and the organization.
- Participant and empowerment skills can form community.

More research on participant-driven services and empowerment

- Community Empowerment: Making Neighborhoods Stronger, Phil Bartle, Community Empowerment Collective, cec.vcn.bc.ca/cmp/modules/emp-ce.htm

Books

- *Strategies for Community Empowerment: Direct Action and Transformative Approaches to Social Change Practice*, Mark G. Hanna. Mellen Press (1994).
- *Soul Consciousness: A New Vision of Community Empowerment and Cultural Transformation*, Stephan Vick. Xlibris US (2019).

Chapter 3:
CAN I TRUST YOU?
Trust

To build and maintain trust we must consistently demonstrate honesty and integrity in our speech and actions.

Richard Riche, oneclearmessage.com

***Trust:** Assured reliance on the character, ability, strength, or truth of someone or something.*

Merriam-Webster Dictionary

Trust is our internal compass, one that helps us to navigate through emotional waters with principle. We can blindly trust persons and situations. However, we are at risk of losing the parts of ourselves that matter most to us. We want to become more conscious of how to build trust and use it to the betterment of others and ourselves. This allows us to have a higher level of safety and integrity. Trust is a primary and important value.

Ideally, trust starts within yourself and moves outward. Trust is crucial in every human relationship and business model. The vital qualities of trust apply to this entire book. Without trust we would never consider calculated risks or be willing to take someone at their word. And your company may not be able to weather internal or external storms. It's hard to get anywhere, including making money, without a degree of trust.

Trust is so essential that, without it, it would be difficult to breathe life into a project that's useful to your stakeholders. It would be like building a house without windows. Trust allows us to have space in a relationship to explore, to tell the truth, and to create an understanding based on respecting one another. Successful business can be lasting if the relationships are based on trust.

It would be problematic to try empowering someone without being trustworthy. If you eliminate trust-building throughout the stages of creating and running a business venture, you're unlikely to sustain your progress and results. Or, at the very least, you'll be labeled a cutthroat and people will avoid you. For-profit business needs to make sure their sales tactics are all aboveboard or eventually people will not place trust in the company.

We shape trust by actions, integrity, and through implementing ideals. We develop it by doing what we say we are going to do, in the manner we said, and in the time frame we committed to. Trust is a powerful force. It is a critical and yet complex principle to apply.

Generally speaking, trust can be developed in an existing relationship and can be applied to challenging circumstances. It's all about developing a rapport between you and others. "Trusting one another involves a gamble—whether it is letting your guard down in a marriage or trusting the behavior of fellow citizens during a pandemic," said Northwestern University psychology professor Dr. Eli Finkel in a recent *New York Times* article. (See end of chapter for resources.)

Realize that it is not important to have all the qualities of trust. Otherwise, it would be the only thing you'd accomplish with your days. Start by advancing a few of trust's merits and concentrate on putting these in practice.

Building a model of trust

- Primary Qualities of Trust: Honesty/integrity, willingness to take calculated risks, consistency (following through), competence, faith in oneself, transparency, humility, internal controls, compassion, accountability, developing one's emotional intelligence, and understanding that people are human and not perfect.
- Secondary Qualities of Trust: Strong problem-solving skills, letting go of control, keeping promises to others, open communications, authenticity, strong moral and ethical principles, willingness to hear opposing ideas, confidence, learning from mistakes, fostering cooperation, exercising good judgment, apologizing when wrong or making a mistake.
- Workforce Qualities of Trust: Encouraging an environment of open exchange of dialogue and ideas, contributing to solutions, being loyal, facing issues directly and openly, having appropriate confidence in others, depending on contracts, making others feel valued, being a helpful role model, knowing your subject matter, acknowledging the nuances and difficulties of building trust.

Instructions for a gingerbread trust person:

Imagine a gingerbeard person.

Inside the gingerbread person, add the ingredients from elements listed above and/or insert your own. Give this gingerbread person the qualities of trust you most value. Keep it to a dozen for each one. Create one for work and one for home. Use this exercise to develop your synergy of trust.

Process gingerbread exercise

What are the most essential qualities of trust for you?

- What aspects of trust do you try to honor at home? At work?
- Why do you think there are differences in the way you trust at home and work? Describe this difference.
- Which of these characteristics of trust presents the most challenge? Why?
- Why do you think trust is skill-based?
- How are you developing trust overall in your life?

"Transparent communications are the foundation for building trust, and consistent action is the glue." says Richard Riche on oneclearmessage.com. Trust is skill-based and requires daily practice. Trust also works on a continuum and can change over time. There are different kinds of trust for different places in our existence. Not all relationships are at the same level.

Apply common sense and know that it is essential that we trust people to different degrees. What follows are possibilities and not exact models to follow. They are meant to give you some ideas on how trust works.

Basic trust: This degree of trust is most often work-related

- Trust acts in a formalized system. (Accountability, consistency, honesty, reliability, commitment, competency, etc.)
- Trust makes or breaks an organizational culture. (Accountability)
- Trust uses rules and contracts. (Accountability)
- At work we ensure one party can trust another to hold up his end of an agreement. (Accountability, reliability, competence, commitment, and honesty/integrity)
- Others can count on you to do your job. (Accountability, reliability commitment, honesty)
- Policies and procedures provide boundaries for how we interact with and treat each other. (Reliability can build cooperation and transparency)
- If we violate business rules, usually there are negative consequences involved. (Accountability)
- Trust depends on teamwork and interconnectedness to get the job done. (Honesty, competency, transparency, accountability, open communications, cooperation, loyalty, agreements)
- If authentic friendships form at work, then we develop the next level of trust, which is everyday trust or intimate trust, depending on the relationship.

Everyday trust: This level is useful with acquaintances at work or in social interactions with friends and associates

- One applies good judgment, accountability, open exchange, and consistency to discern if a person is worthy of trust.
- Only when you see that this person has reached a certain point of honesty, integrity, follow-through, and consistency is she to be trusted. (Generates cooperation, confidence, exercises good judgment, makes others feel valued)
- The person trusts you and seeks your ideas.
- Additionally, a person demonstrates genuine compassion and concern.
- A person who is trustworthy tells the truth, follows through, and does what he says he is going to. (Consistency, honesty, reliability)
- Both parties' expectations align with each other. (Open exchange of dialogue makes others feel valued, provides a good example, generates cooperation, exercises good judgment, is consistent)

Intimate trust: This level of trust is the deepest and is applied to close friends, spouses, partners, and family

- These attributes of trust are reserved for the most significant people in our lives, such as a life partner, family, and/or close friends. (Faith in oneself and others, compassion, accountability, taking calculated risks, honesty/integrity, letting go of controlling another person)

- These trust elements mean you share hopes, dreams, goals, ambitions, fears, and doubts. (Honesty, reliability, authenticity, willing to hear opposing ideas, confidence, learning from mistakes)
- Your level of transparency and vulnerability can increase because you realize you are not going to be taken advantage of.
- You've proven to those close to you that you possess loyalty, exercise good judgment, and have strong moral/ethical principles. You are trustworthy as the other person close to you is also honorable.

Another quote from Dr. Eli Finkel sums it up: "Trust is a willingness to allow yourself to be vulnerable with the hope that life will be better for having done so." (See end of chapter for resources.)

How trust functions with participant-driven services

Building trust is a value that can be organically integrated into daily transactions with others. I recommend becoming more conscious of whom and when we trust, because it can aid the development of participant-driven services tenfold with awareness.

Trust affects both empowerment, and subsequently, participant-driven services. You need this particular composition to solidify community-forming work. By reaching out and involving the community in selecting services, allowing them to act as your advisor, and talking through the proposed philosophy with them, you are accomplishing real steps in building trusting relationships.

In for-profit business, it is vital that trust is developed in the workplace. It doesn't necessitate having a deep level of trust for your teammates (which might be inappropriate). Yet, work relationships with others need to encompass selected trust ingredients. These might include understanding your interconnectedness to others at the organization, possessing good judgment, cooperation, telling the truth, and having consistency and accountability (among other trust characteristics).

For-profit companies are encouraged to consider (in one form or another) these applications. They are powerful relationship-building tools that foster unity, which can lead to achievement.

Building participant-driven services with trust

- Have authentic, honest interactions.
- Ensure consistency/reliability. Do what you say you are going to do and when you say you are going to do it.
- Share and advance community leadership as appropriate.
- Positively acknowledge members' involvement regularly.
- Role model the behavior you want from others.
- Stay open to conflicting ideas.
- Apply the concept of transparency to all community meetings.
- Problem-solve with the community.
- Create a culture where anyone can learn from his mistakes.
- Let go of control.

"Trust takes a long time and effort to develop but only one event to diminish or to eliminate it completely."

Why Trust Matters in the Workplace, Insightlink.com

The next integral step in acquiring trust with the community is to take suitable action and communicate progress or obstacles. Establish an environment of trust that fosters constructive bonds. This is where communication, consistency, reliability, commitment, and follow-through are fundamental to building trust.

Additionally, when you're under the directive of the community, make sure to give credit where credit is due. Use community members as leaders and guides. For example, if someone has volunteered her time to have members sign up for the advisory board, it's valuable to mention her contribution and the gratitude that's due.

Volunteering without getting paid is unfortunately not always acknowledged. It is key, if you want to engage volunteers/supporters, that you understand and recognize their contributions. Become the Pied Piper. Get people excited to be on the ground floor of generating the services or goods people want and will use.

This is where the rubber meets the road. You must be able to act upon what you have learned and relate it to the services or products requested. The next step could be to distribute a timeline for when services are expected to begin. Most significantly, communicate with everyone who has been involved, and make sure they know what actions you are going to take and when.

Think about trust

- What does trust look like at your business? What would you like it to be?

- How would you go about building trust with services, particularly participant-driven services?
- What are one or two things you can do to improve trust in your workplace?
- Why is trust so important?
- Why do you think trust is such a challenge to achieve?
- Where might you begin to build trust in the establishment you serve?

You're right!

We were fortunate to have had the opportunity to buy our building in 2000 and renovate the additional 2,500-square-foot space we acquired in 2002. It's no laughing matter when you live right next door to a significant improvement project. There was an excessive amount of noise and dust for nearly a year. The great news was that we doubled our ability to serve the community. I was excited to see how people responded to it.

However, just days after we opened the new space, I realized our Chinese moms and grandmas had gathered in a group and were discussing something with passion, but not the happy kind. I asked one of the teachers who spoke the language what they were talking about. She didn't want to say but eventually relented and told me, "They think the new program space is stuffy."

A lot of renovation dollars and a brand-new ventilation (HVAC) system later, I recognized that they were spot on. A few weeks later, I was sitting in the staff kitchen and looking into our new program space. I noticed there was what appeared to be a large piece of glass just above the handicapped door.

I imagined that we could replace it with a window that opened to allow in fresh air. As luck would have it, we had a glass guy nearby. He custom-made and installed an affordable window that opened when needed to the outside. I was thrilled, and so were all the people who were attending programs in our new room.

I trusted (and agreed) that participants in our programs needed better air circulation in the space. I was motivated to find an appropriate solution to their concerns. I wanted to demonstrate that their voices mattered and simultaneously meet their needs.

Empowerment along with trust is the foundation that holds the concepts and values of creating and building a healthy community. The component needed to do this is building trust with your employees and constituents. It is a mindset and a lens through which to look at the world that sets you apart from the crowded field of business.

For-profit trust ideas to put into practice

- Trust builds a solid foundation within the company on which to work from. Begin a conversation on trust to see what kind of environment you have.
- Trust matters because it can build solid relationships that can help you connect with others.
- Create an environment in which people can thrive and speak up with confidence.

Nonprofit trust opportunities

- Lead off with trust when you want to build community.
- To start to build trust, make sure you do what is promised, particularly for the designated area.
- All trust is relationship based. Know the different levels and what kind of trust is appropriate to use in the workplace.

More research on trust

- "13 Simple Strategies for Building Trust," Carthage Buckley, liveyourtruestory.com
- Dr. Eli Finkel, a psychology professor at Northwestern University, quoted in "New Honor System on Masks: Am I to Trust These People?" *New York Times*, May 18, 2021, nyt.com
- "5 Elements for Building Trust in the Workplace," Richard Riche, oneclearmessage.com
- "Leading with Trust," Randy Conley, kenblanchard.com
- "Cultivating Trust Is Critical and Surprisingly Complex," Kent Grayson, insight.kellogg.northwestern.edu
- "The 3 Elements of Trust," Jack Zenger and Joseph Folkman, Harvard Business Review, February 5, 2019, https://hbr.org/2019/02/the-3-elements-of-trust
- "How the Best Leaders Build Trust," Stephen M.R. Covey, https://www.leadershipnow.com/CoveyOnTrust.html

Books

- *The Art of Community: Seven Principles for Belonging*, Charles H. Vogl. Berrett-Koehler Publishers (2016).
- *The Thin Book of Trust: An Essential Primer for Building Trust at Work*, Charles Feltman. Thin Book Publishing (2008).

Chapter 4:
A MAP NAVIGATES DIRECTION
Community Maps

"The greatest thing in this world is not so much where we stand, as in what direction we are moving."

Oliver Wendell Holmes

Community Mapping: *Community Mapping refers to the process of collecting data that identifies assets, or resources, within a defined area.*

Maps for Community Organizing, https://hc-v6-static.s3.amazonaws.com/media/resources/tmp/Community_Organizing.pdf

Community mapping is a cataloguing of a community's strengths (assets). It is the process of figuring out the constructive resources available to a neighborhood or group. It includes taking stock of public (institutions), community, and individual supports. This can be a positive reality for nonprofits and for-profits alike.

For clarifying purposes, community asset mapping can be divided into three main categories. According to The Community Mapping Toolkit (Preston City Council, https://ucanr.edu/sites/CA4-HA/files/206668.pdf), they include "the individual (e.g., skills, talents, gifts, abilities, knowledge, etc.), the community (e.g., social, groups, teams, associations, voluntary, cultural, etc.) and intuitions (e.g., business, libraries, schools, facilities, housing, parks, infrastructure, etc.)."

Community mapping was the first strategy implemented as our nonprofit secured the funding from the state in the summer of 1993. I applied this technique informally. It was an initial way to understand the community. It was also a technique to start to develop participation from the community by identifying and working with its strengths.

I don't remember how I found out about John McKnight and his inspired work on community mapping and neighborhood development. But I am so happy I did. (See more about his work at johnmcknightabcdinstitute.weebly.com.) At the core of this philosophy is empowerment.

McKnight's early days as a community organizer helped him understand how the community can function best from a grassroots level on up. McKnight noted that his colleagues' and his research had promoted an understanding of the usefulness of local resources, capacities, and relationships through a tool called Asset Based Community Development (ABCD). The emphasis is on individuals and the power they can bring to the community. It is genuinely inspiring.

We applied these basic principles by walking the neighborhood and making notes on all of the strengths. I saw a branch library, well-maintained homes, two large public parks, a community health center, and three public schools.

Little did I know at the time, I was just touching the tip of the iceberg of community mapping. Dan Duncan, a senior consultant of Clear Impact, the Asset Based Community Development Institute created a toolkit for community asset mapping.

"Asset-based community development (ABCD) is John McKnight's and colleagues' work for the sustainable development of communities based on their strengths and potentials. It involves assessing the resources, skills, and experience available in a community, organizing the community around issues that move its members into action, and then determining and taking appropriate action." (See "Maps for Community Organizing," https://clearimpact.com/resources/publications/asset-mapping-toolkit/.)

John McKnight and John Kretzmann co-authored a book in 1993 called *Building Communities from the Inside Out: A Path Toward Finding and Mobilizing a Community's Assets.* This book outlined their asset-based approach to community development. Its foundation of the community mapping strategy rests on a few remarkable and simple truths.

1. *Everyone has gifts.*
2. *Everyone has something to contribute.*
3. *Everyone cares about something, and that passion is his or her motivation to act.*

Overall, what I found out through community mapping was that the neighborhood I was serving was, and still is, a "working-class," multicultural area. In the early 90's it was changing rapidly and becoming an immigrant, primarily Asian, community.

My positive findings of the community mapping process (ABCD)

- A high-performing public neighborhood–based elementary school
- A public middle school
- A significantly large public high school
- A considerable recreation and park site that would include a sizeable playground and clubhouse
- A public library (branch)
- A municipal health center
- A major thoroughfare in and out of the city
- A group of residents, some who grew up in the neighborhood
- Many homeowners with families and a commitment to a healthy community in which to live and raise their children

The challenges I found with community mapping (ABCD)

- Safety issues from drive-by shootings
- Protection concerns from other forms of violence
- Robberies
- Muggings
- Gangs
- Boarded-up storefronts along the main street
- Graffiti on most of the stores
- These challenges were invisible and unknown to City Hall

Weighing the positives and negatives, I felt the scales tipped in favor of working with and empowering residents with their many strengths. The critical parts we discussed were how to empower the community to become involved in the community mapping process and start realizing and building upon what their community assets were.

Residents can learn to develop, lean on, and support these positive attributes.

Although I initially used community mapping for myself to determine whether this project could succeed, I highly recommend that you involve members of the community in this early stage. That way, you can set the expectations and tone for both participant-driven services and leadership from within the community you are serving.

Think about these questions before you use asset-based community development (ABCD)

- Reflect on your approach to forming community and what the literature is describing. Can you use a version of asset mapping that suits your purposes?
- Are you willing to invest the time needed to do asset-based community development?
- Have you determined what you are hoping to learn and how to get there?
- How and when do you want to involve potential participants?
- Why or why not might community mapping work for your business?

As previously mentioned, you do not have to follow the exact process of ABCD community mapping to get reliable results concerning a community's assets. While using a toolkit is a comprehensive and helpful way to understand the main themes of the area, it is time-consuming. It doesn't have to be so. An abbreviated process can be applied for these specific purposes as long as you can keep it unbiased and neutral in tone.

Call to action (ABCD)

Do your research. Find an ABCD toolkit or information on how to apply asset mapping. Modify if appropriate to fit your purpose. It doesn't have to be exact to be a powerful tool in community development.

1. Identify potential participants who can help you recognize what resources are in the community.
2. Once you have identified participants, ask them to get involved and use their talents to solve issues in the community by mapping its strengths and weakness. (This can include any area of services. It can be a community of disabled, homeless, war veterans, etc.)
3. Create an asset map timeline and a brief job description for community folks. Clarify expectations regarding time commitments.
4. Help people determine the broad categories they will need for community mapping. "General categories could include associations, physical space, institutions, schools, individuals and the local economy," according to resources.depaul.edu/abcd-institute.
5. Gather all the resources you will need for success however you are defining it.

6. Get ready, get set, and go out with your team and figure out what your assets are in the community.
7. Assets can be divided into individual, community, and institutional.
8. Evaluate and analyze the data.
9. Celebrate your accomplishments in a way that's meaningful for the participants and speaks to the worthiness of the project.

For-profit community mapping ideas to put into practice

- Apply principles of asset-based development toward learning about your customers.
- Asset mapping can aid in discovering an appropriate direction in which to move, which in the long run can save time and money.
- These strategies recognize assets *and* potential problems.

Nonprofit community mapping opportunities

- Community mapping is a primary empowerment strategy. Harnessing this approach can help you know the community and energize the very individuals who can support your efforts.
- Community mapping helps identify where the skills and talents are in a particular area.
- It is easier to begin work when you know the landscape and have realistic expectations.

More research on community mapping

- "Participatory Asset Mapping: A Community Research Lab Toolkit," https://communityscience.com/wp-content/uploads/2021/04/AssetMappingToolkit.pdf
- "Maps for Community Organizing," https://clearimpact.com/resources/publications/asset-mapping-toolkit/
- "Community Mapping for Health Equity Advocacy," Sarah Treuhaft, Policy Link, June 2009, https://www.policylink.org/sites/default/files/Community_Mapping_for_Health_Equity_Treuhaft.pdf
- "The Community Mapping Toolkit," Preston City Council, https://ucanr.edu/sites/CA4-HA/files/206668.pdf

Books

- *Building Communities from the Inside Out: A Path Toward Finding and Mobilizing a Community's Assets*, John Kretzmann and John McKnight. ACTA Publications (1993).
- *Qualitative Research Methods for Community Development*, Robert Mark Silverman and Kelly L. Patterson. Routledge (2014).
- *The Abundant Community: Awakening the Power of Families and Neighborhoods*, Peter Block and John McKnight. Berrett-Koehler Publishers (2012).

Chapter 5:
PEOPLE ARE KEY
Community Advisory Boards

"Tell me and I forget, teach me and I remember, involve me and I learn."

Benjamin Franklin

Community Advisory Board: *A community advisory board is a group of community members and organization representatives that provide community information and assistance to the resources project or initiative.*

West Virginia Clinical and Transactional Science Institute, wvtsi.org

Creating and establishing a community advisory board is an exciting and significant process. This is the second action I took to understand community needs when I started the nonprofit. It is a variation on the theme of empowering people to help shape the work.

Most of us want to know the pros and cons involved before we launch a major new initiative. Advisory boards can help forecast the success of any given project.

My example of the central role of the community advisory board follows in a story format.

A noteworthy community board

I had help selecting people for this first advisory board from my teacher and administrator friends at the Bay Elementary School. They assisted me in identifying folks who:

- weren't afraid to tell it like it is,
- committed to being part of the process (and the monthly meetings),
- were passionate about the neighborhood, and
- represented the multicultural population.

People on the community board represented the major ethnicities at the school and in the neighborhood. They were African American, Filipino, Chinese, Vietnamese, Hispanic, and Caucasian. It was a diverse mix of about twenty people who regularly attended monthly meetings.

Some participants were new to the neighborhood, and a handful had grown up in the area. Yet they were all on the same page about wanting to engage with processes that facilitated an improved neighborhood environment.

Many brought their children to the evening meetings when it worked best for the majority of participants. Childcare became a necessity. Food was served, but the advisory board parents decided to feature various foods from the cultures present.

Teams of people from the same ethnicity made mouthwatering regional dishes. Residents outdid themselves, and a good-natured competition ensued. It resulted in shared recipes at the end of the meeting. Although it wasn't designed to do so, this shared food activity strengthened bonds between participants and created the very community we were seeking.

I am not sure whether food, participants, or both were the productive elements, but the board developed into a force to reckon with. Their mantra became: "Make the neighborhood a safer place to raise children."

The board lasted three years, with many of the original members maintaining their attendance. Some advisory board members went on to become great resources as our services and programs took shape.

Additionally, community advisory board contributors were instrumental in selecting questions for our needs assessment. They had original ideas that added depth and dimension to the research tool. The results from five hundred surveys led directly to our initial service offerings.

Advisory board members said they were proud to be part of the planning. The dialogue was fun and upbeat. Yet it often turned serious when discussing the threats posed to the neighborhood by safety issues and crimes.

Empowering community members on the advisory board

Community advisory board members (CABM):

- Identified strengths and skills that they were willing to share in the formation of new services for the neighborhood
- Identified neighborhood assets that could add to their quality of life
- Determined the questions for the community needs assessment
- Helped begin the first services
- Intuitively used food to break barriers in a nonthreatening way
- Offered free childcare so parents could attend meetings

General steps to set up a community advisory board

- Be clear at the outset about what your goals are for having an advisory board. Simultaneously, start identifying potential members.
- Form a partnership first with supporters who are recommended and represent different interests and diversity of all sorts: ages, cultures, length of time in the neighborhood, and so on, and ask them to be participants on the board.
- Make sure community advisory board members understand that this is not a governing board/board of directors but vested parties working in an advisory capacity.
- Set a time limit on the meeting. Accomplish what you need to within the set time frame.

- If you are interested in continuing with some members, ask the appropriate volunteers to help with a variety of functions that may include funding, lobbying, and input on additional programs.

Specific steps for creating a community advisory board

- Create advisory board job descriptions.
- Recruit advisory board members.
- Brainstorm ground rules with advisory board participants. Post them at every meeting.
- Generate and keep an updated timeline for meetings with potential activities for advisory members.
- Make certain that action items happen and include the outcomes in a report back to your advisory group.
- Set term limits for members. It may be anything from three months to three years.
- Decide who will facilitate the advisory board monthly meetings. Is it a staff person or an advisory board member?
- Build trust as you go through this process.
- Include childcare and meals (often necessary for parents' attendance).
- Make space to talk about trying or unforeseen issues (e.g., charging for programs when you thought everything was going to be free). These updates and discussions can occur at your monthly advisory board meetings, in a group email, or through another methodology.

Anything missing? Every community is different. Add to this list as needed.

For-profit advisory board ideas to put into practice

- Use people you develop a bond with to co-vet products or services you are thinking about offering.
- Advisory boards are a type of market research that is economical and trustworthy.
- Use ground rules during meetings to help develop an environment of trust.

Nonprofit business community advisory board opportunities

- Treat the advisory board members as the special advisors to the project. If possible, provide meals, childcare, and other amenities your community deems necessary.
- Make certain the community advisory board ideas are talked about and implemented whenever possible.
- Report back to your advisory board any decisions that may affect them and/or services being offered.

More research on community advisory boards

- "Roles and Responsibilities of Advisory Boards," Hildy Gotllieb, 2009, http://www.help4nonprofits.com/UseItToday/UseItToday-Roles_of_Advisory_Boards.htm
- "Nonprofit Advisory Boards: Why They Matter and How to Get Them Off the Ground," MissionBox Global Network, 2021, https://www.missionbox.com/article/59/nonprofit-advisory-boards-why-they-matter-how-to-get-them-off-the-ground

Books

- *Community Advisory Board: Practical Tools for Self-Assessment, 2nd ed.*, Gerardus Blokdyk. 5STARCooks (2018).

Chapter 6:
UNCOVER THE ISSUES
Community Needs Assessments

"Alone, we can do so little, together we can do so much."

Helen Keller

Community Needs Assessments: *Community needs assessments seek to gather accurate information representative of the needs of a community. Assessments are performed before taking action and are used to determine current situations and identify issues for action. Needs assessments establish the essential foundation for vital planning.*

learningtogive.org

Addressing the needs

Community needs assessment is a practical way to survey people to find out what they think about something your company wants to do. It can establish a helpful feedback loop, give a clear direction on a course of action to take, and find out details about the particular environment you are working in. It is a great way to form invaluable partnerships.

A third and final significant strategy I used to develop empowerment and determine our first services was distributing a five-hundred person community survey. The survey addressed the central themes I most wanted to cover. Once I received the responses, I moved into the next phase of establishing services.

The community advisory board worked on the survey questions with me. Of the 750 surveys sent out, we received 500 back. The secret to getting so many assessments returned was to distribute them to the neighborhood elementary school we had grown out of. I also offered an incentive for returned surveys.

At that time, there were 750 students in the neighborhood school. I gave a free pizza party to the class that returned the most surveys from their parents. To say this was a successful strategy is an understatement. It brought out competition in the best of them. A handful of the surveys were even filled out by the fifth-grade students.

The research was specifically geared to the audience I most wanted to reach and receive input from. We were trying to eliminate child abuse. It made sense to survey a neighborhood elementary school population to discover the resources and support that parents felt were essential in raising healthy children.

The particular tool we engaged our population with was a comprehensive, four-page needs assessment. I had a template from the Mayor's Office of Community Services and permission to use it.

We treated these research questions as a launching pad for discussions with the advisory board on what matters and information to include. When the surveys were filled out, it gave us a clear direction on where we needed to head regarding programs and services

Why a community needs assessment is valuable

1. People become aware of what's happening in the community and can give feedback on potential new resources.
2. It establishes the all-important feedback loop that you need in forming participant-driven services.
3. It gives people at the helm of the project a clear direction to take from the very beginning. This is vital to the success of your organization's planning efforts and can be an excellent step in the right direction.

Think about community needs assessment

- Do we have questions on the community needs assessment that get at the purpose for establishing services? How is this done?
- Is this query framed appropriately for the community?
- Are the questions clear? Could they be misconstrued?
- Do we have the right inquiries to understand the strengths in the local area?
- Are we asking about safety, people's satisfaction in the neighborhood, whether there are enough city services, and if the public schools are supportive (e.g., is there a pre-k, after-school program, free or low-cost lunches, etc.)?
- Are we asking what people's biggest concerns are regarding the community?

- Are we asking people's opinions on what most of the resources should be allocated to?
- Are we questioning other areas people would have the most interest in?

Hint: It's helpful to have a laundry list of things you can cover so participants can pick their top three.

The big reveal

The survey I gave participants included a brief disclaimer. This stipulation set out the parameters of potential program areas we could provide via our funding source, the State of California. Also, the Office of Child Abuse Prevention had general expectations regarding how we could spend grant monies (e.g., serving families and creating community with these families). I included this information concisely in the survey.

In the needs assessment, residents were encouraged to say what they needed and wanted in their community, i.e., the services and programs. And they responded. The needs assessment gave us another map in creating our first services.

It's interesting because as diverse as this neighborhood was, people were united in their responses. Across the board, they wanted to see their area get the same level of services that more affluent communities in the Bay Area were receiving.

The survey also showed that residents wanted an increase in safety services since there was spillover violence from surrounding neighborhoods. Lastly, neighbors wanted local city governments to fund nonprofits serving communities, which they felt could make a substantial difference for years to come.

From these surveys, people requested parent-child activities. Our first endeavor in this realm was making valentines cards on the actual

Valentine's Day. We offered all the supplies needed. The fledging center was virtually strewn with tiny glittering hearts from floor to ceiling.

In addition to parent-child activities, we added nutrition classes from UC Davis, California; parenting classes; exercise sessions; an English as a Second Language program five days a week, twice a day; and an ongoing series of How to Be Safe in Your Community workshops.

I was incredibly grateful to the participants who engaged so completely with the community needs assessments, community mapping, and community advisory boards. Four months after starting the center, we were able to retain an impressive group of neighborhood people who helped generate processes and assessments that led to the participant-driven services people wanted.

Community Needs Assessment: True or False

1. The needs assessment survey should be as short as possible.
   Answer: True or false. It is all relative. Some would consider my initial survey of four pages front and back too long. However, it was just right for our community and provided the information I was looking for. The trick is creating the proper length survey for your specific audience. It is smart to offer a small incentive, whether it is a nutrition bar or a magnet, with the organization's name (or something else of your choosing).

2. It may be appropriate to ask questions in the needs assessment about the quality of life in adjoining neighborhoods.
   Answer: False. In my experience, you do not want to muddy the waters and ask questions about another neighborhood. You have neither the time nor space to do so.

3. People are very hesitant to fill out a needs assessment survey.
   Answer: False. Potential participants who I worked with were not hesitant to fill out the surveys. They were anxious

to improve the neighborhood. We also had permission to distribute the surveys at the school. Whenever possible, use groups of people who know the work of the organization you are representing.

4. Making the survey anonymous is not recommended because you want to capture as many people as you can who can become part of the organization down the line.
   Answer: True. You want to make the survey anonymous, so people feel as comfortable as possible filling out the questionnaires as honestly as they can.

5. It's not worth going through the work of putting together a survey if you don't get at least two hundred respondents.
   Answer: True or false. Again, it depends on how you plan to use the survey. If a higher number of participants is needed, then you must think through how you will reach your goal. The critical factor is to be as transparent as possible.

In the first five years of pulling the center together, I used surveys frequently. These assessments gathered essential information and led to impressive results. However, once you've gathered the information, you must be willing to act upon it.

For instance, if you want to start an after-school program for children and you send out a questionnaire to many parents who need this service, do not disregard the data. Start an after-school program with the information you gleaned.

If feedback from the parents says they are solely interested in their children attending an after-school enrichment program, then your job is to create and focus on an enrichment program for children. This process is empowering for future participants if you follow through as a service provider that fulfills their requests.

Pay attention, and people will tell you what they want, and what they need the supports (i.e., programs, services, and goods) to look like. At the end of the day, give people what they desire. Do something concrete toward this goal and communicate it to your audience. And be transparent, whatever techniques you use. If you do, you are almost guaranteeing participants will be there and attend programs or services (or buy things) you offer.

Stakeholders will come to see that this entire process of participant-driven services will benefit them. Use these empowering approaches to create a network of active contributors who will become an invaluable asset to your nonprofit or company. It is a productive approach to establishing a powerful sense of belonging and connection.

For-profit community needs assessment ideas to put into practice

- Surveys can give concrete feedback and direction.
- Guarantee involvement in your services or products by involving potential buyers in meaningful ways.
- Think of needs assessment as a type of market research. You need this information to know how to best proceed with your rollout of the new or improved product or service.

Nonprofit community needs assessment opportunities

- You can use small incentives to get a big bang for your buck for returned surveys.
- With pinpointed questions, surveys can support planning efforts in moving in the right direction.
- Make surveys anonymous since it helps ensure people will offer honest feedback.

More Research on Community Needs Assessment

- "Community Needs Assessments," Tracy Taylor and Mackenzie Brunson, https://www.learningtogive.org/resources/community-needs-assessments
- "How to Conduct a Community Needs Assessment," https://www.galaxydigital.com/blog/community-needs-assessment/
- "Four Key Strategies for Successful Community Needs Assessment Surveys," November 2019, https://blog.publicinput.com/community-needs-assessment-survey
- "Needs Assessment, Definition, Overview and Examples," Indeed Editorial Team, 2021, https://www.indeed.com/career-advice/career-development/needs-assessment

Books

- *The Community Needs Assessment Workbook*, Rodney A. Wambeam. Oxford University Press (2015).
- *A Practical Guide to Needs Assessment (American Society for Training and Development) 3rd Edition*, Catherine Sleezer, Darlene F. Russ-Eft, and Kavita Gupta. John Wiley & Sons Inc. (2014).

Chapter 7:
REACH OUT
Outreach

Many of life's failures are people who did not realize how close they were to success.

Thomas Edison

Outreach: *Extending of services or assistance beyond current or usual limit. The activity or process of bringing information or services to people.*

Merriam-Webster Dictionary, merriam-webster.com

Outreach

"No man is an island" is a philosophy that can pertain to outreach. It is a deliberate, straightforward, people-oriented and indispensable concept for business. Outreach spreads your message by packaging it in a way that makes sense to your audience. It helps folks to know what you are offering. In other words, it's a type of advertising. When you talk about your work, your values should be front and center.

You can present excellent programs or goods, but without people, the work becomes pointless. Also, you'd never attract business or make money. Organizations require that we bring attention to our services or products. The best way to master this function is through outreach (or, if you prefer, advertising or marketing).

The most direct way to accomplish this goal is through relationship building. It is a key component of outreach. Making significant relationships through reaching out to others can allow an organization to fulfill whatever its purpose is.

The strategies involved in outreach should be multiple in scope and include responsible content combined with an intent that you are cultivating an awareness of your company and what it offers.

Outreach is a necessity

Some years ago, a staff person named Billy wanted to put on a health fair for current participants and the surrounding community. I had a lot of experience, mostly single-handedly putting on wellness events in the early days of the nonprofit.

Community members enjoy health fairs and love all the "freebies" that come with them. In theory, at least, it's a great idea. However, health fairs are time-intensive and a crapshoot as to how many people will attend. It is challenging to get the providers that have the most significant draw (e.g., hearing, vision, cholesterol, diabetes testing, etc.) and finding the right day and time for the highest participant attendance.

If health is the primary function of your business, then put on a health fair. But when health is a bonus service, it's not worth all the time and energy necessary to put on a great wellness event and have a strong turnout. That's especially so, given that time is at a premium in any business. Billy and I went multiple rounds about the pros and cons of hosting the event. In the end, I gave him my okay and hoped for the best.

Billy felt strongly about offering the health fair to the community and went about recruiting health care advocates and screeners. And while he had obtained first-rate providers, he had few participants. Billy offered the health fair in the late afternoon on a weekday when the after-school program was in session and parents were picking up their kids. Unfortunately, many more potential participants and members of the community were still at work.

I had some trepidation about the chosen time, which was not optimal. In addition, I also felt outreach was lacking internally (to existing participants) and externally (to community members). This contributed to the fact that hardly anyone showed up.

Most businesses have stories like these. People have great ideas, but the outreach performance falls short of strong attendance. This can indicate that there was not enough outreach (marketing) to make the event worthwhile. How do you avoid the problems of low participation when you know that people would get a lot out of what you are offering?

I believe brainstorming the potential challenges of outreach from the outset and doing something about it can make a big difference. If you don't have the expertise to know what the problems might be, seek out a partner or someone in your broader community who does.

How to excel at outreach

- Formalize your outreach strategies. Decide the best way for your business to advertise and bring people to the services. Who's the best employee to handle outreach (or is there a designated department)?
- Create an outreach committee among employees. The committee's responsibility would be to handle all things related to outreach. If your company is too small for a committee or you don't want to take that route, use what works from the ideas given and keep them as your outreach/marketing approach.
- Brainstorm and strategize successful outreach tactics. Make a list of all your current outreach strategies, including external and internal ones. Have staff rate what's working and what's not, and then focus your efforts on what's working. What outreach method would make the most sense for your products or services?

  Possible outreach strategies to apply to your work:

- Advertise. The ways to advertise are almost endless.
- Post on multiple digital communication platforms to reach your participants.
- Split advertising and its costs with outside program or corporate partners.
- Utilize community bulletin boards, both virtual and real.
- Word of mouth.
- Put flyers on nearby business storefronts (with their permission).
- Provide incentives for people who attend.
- Use foot traffic (if you're located in an area that draws a lot of people).

- Tap into email and social media to connect to potential groups. Become a social influencer.
- At special events, hand out information about the other programs, services, and/or goods that you offer.

There are many more ideas! Please add to this list.

Review outreach/marketing plans regularly. What works with one event, product, or program doesn't necessarily work as well with another. Innovate. Be willing to change your approaches.

As you experiment, track how well a particular outreach tactic is working. Can the strategy be improved, or is it time to try something else? Make regular recommendations for improvements to outreach methodologies.

Outreach can be incredibly inventive. It helps people know about the resources in their community and in a broader area. It's good to have numerous strategies in your arsenal. As previously mentioned, outreach is marketing, and it's about getting the word out about nonprofit service opportunities.

Outreach in reverse directions

It was 1994, and we had just finished the first renovations to our rental property with Habitat for Humanity, adding offices and classrooms. The friendly neighborhood librarian Samantha approached me on the playground at our partner school. She said the city library had been on a month-to-month lease for many years. They received notification that they had thirty days to vacate the premises. She was frantic to find space, for obvious reasons.

The librarians were getting ready to start their summer reading programs, and many community children depended on them for fun summertime literacy activities. She asked if the library could share our space for a few months. We had just that week moved back to our newly customized site.

I asked her to give me a day to think about it. Funnily enough, I heard my mom's voice in my head saying, "What's to think about? You have space, and they need some." I was completely engrossed in reading and spent many happy childhood hours in libraries, so this sounded like a great idea to me.

I called Samantha the next day and told her we were in. She moved into the classrooms in the next few weeks with crates full of books, tons of stickers, and other incentives for their reading program. It was a significant partnership.

We figured out space-sharing without a hitch. Samantha soon moved back to the South, where she grew up, and a new librarian replaced her. She, too, was amiable. The city librarian then asked to remain in our space for the next eighteen months so they could find an appropriate place in the neighborhood and build or refurbish it. At this point, I didn't hesitate to say yes.

They moved into the side of the center we were just starting to use. While they had to share the space with our morning English as a Second Language (ESL) class and other services, they were okay with it. The branch library staff was pleased that they got to stay in the community and work with the people they cared about.

They had limited services and hours, but they still were able to maintain their presence in the neighborhood. It was a fortuitous experience for us at the center. We met numerous people who participated in our programs who had found us by coming to the library. Also, the library paid us rent, and our mutually beneficial partnership prospered for years to come.

I would never have thought that we could have had such a satisfying partnership with an organization such as a citywide library, with all of its regulations. However, the librarians came to us, so they probably didn't want to impose any more restrictions than necessary.

It's essential to stay open to the many remarkable possibilities out there. Outreach is vital to community development and instituting new services. And sometimes those services come to you.

Outreach includes using creativity with the goal of enticing people to participate in your organization's services. Outreach strategies can be ongoing, yet need regular review, as outreach costs money and staff time. Also, an outreach strategy can be just one time for a specific event or need. But outreach in general must happen with great regularity.

An outreach/marketing committee or department is crucial so the responsibility among team members is shared. No one wants outreach to become mundane or, worse, burdensome. If planned, it can elevate your organization to be exceptional for those it serves.

"Necessity is the mother of invention."

Plato

Outreach bonanza!

In the early days, our center was a laboratory of experimentation as we tried to find the right outreach formula to get participants to attend the programs and services, starting with the first Halloween party.

When I moved from Michigan to California, my sweet daughter was only nine years old. We spent the first couple of Halloweens wandering the streets, trying to figure out where it was safe and fun for kids to go trick-or-treating. It's an understatement to say it was a hit-or-miss experience.

The Halloween of 1994 was the first community party at the nonprofit I ran. I distributed flyers at the school and in the neighborhood. I decided that I would entertain kids with art and craft projects and have a costume parade and contest around the center. I also offered goodie bags with a little candy and some healthy snacks.

Others were also concerned about what to do with their children. The first Halloween party was an incredible success, as measured by all the fun kids were having. More than three hundred kids and adults attended. The center was incredibly packed. This party was the basic prototype for all of the other parties held at the center.

Think about outreach by answering these questions

- Do you think of outreach and marketing as the same? If you had to guess, does a marketing department function the same way as an outreach department would?
- How is outreach handled at your company?
- Would you say it's on the chaotic side or more organized?
- Do you think more people would use your services or buy your goods if you had a systematized approach to outreach/marketing?
- Is the time right to set up outreach meetings once a month?

Outreach is communicating with your target audience about your work and how it can operate in their favor. It is Marketing 101. Outreach can help you serve your constituents, which can be a tremendous social benefit to business of all size.

Outreach is putting the word out about what you do. It can give birth to the expansion of your services or goods through helpful marketing options (e.g., building relationships).

Outreach uses various tactics to get the message delivered. Observe which tool functions best and use it. At the same time, continue to research new approaches for your enterprise. Know that outreach is a crucial form of marketing for your products, services, and programs.

For-profit outreach ideas to put into practice

- Understand the nature of sales through outreach. Both come into play by locating and engaging your customers.
- Use social media regularly to influence and inform your consumer base. But don't forget the all-important effort of person-to-person connections.
- Reaching out to potential customers is second nature to staying alive in business, as is making a profit. Keep your successful strategies and let go of those that no longer work.

Nonprofit outreach opportunities

- Outreach is a crucial element of getting the word out about your programs and services.
- One size does not fit all. Develop plenty of outreach strategies that are beneficial for a variety of services, events, and programs.
- Brainstorm creative ideas that target a particular part of your community. You can break up outreach strategies for effectively reaching a more difficult audience.

More research on outreach

- The Community Organizing website, https://comm-org.wisc.edu/about.htm
- "Types of Outreach Marketing for Your Business," https://www.universalclass.com/articles/business/types-of-outreach-marketing-for-your-business.htm
- "How Community Outreach Can Boost Customer Acquisition & Retention," Neil Patel, https://neilpatel.com/blog/community-outreach-boosts-customer-retention/

- "Community Organizing: People Power from the Grass Roots," Dave Beckwith and Christina Lopez, Center for Community Change, 1998, https://www.participatorymethods.org/resource/community-organizing-people-power-grassroots

Books

- *Made to Stick: Why Some Ideas Survive and Others Die*, Chip Heath and Dan Heath. Random House (2007).
- *The Marketer's Guide: How to Sell Everything from Apples to Zippers*, Maziar Jafari. Mazz Jeff (2021).

Chapter 8: MAKING CONNECTIONS *Networking*

"If you want one year of prosperity, grow grain. If you want ten years of prosperity, grow trees. If you want one hundred years of prosperity, grow people."

Chinese proverb

Networking: *The exchange of information or services among individuals, groups, or institutions specifically: the cultivation of productive relationships for employment or business.*

Merriam-Webster Dictionary

Networking

Networking is about making connections with like-minded professionals and other specialized groups. It can be enjoyable and gratifying. It encourages individuals to reach out to others, usually outside of your normal work environment.

Networking examples might include trading expertise, socializing, problem solving, gathering insights, advocacy, and/or setting standards for success. Networking often functions as a companion to outreach. It is also an essential way to learn from others, grow the business, adopt best practices, and engage in enjoyable human contact.

Networking is second nature to humans. We don't even realize how common it is. People network to find dates, jobs, doctors, lawyers, the perfect yoga teacher, and the list goes on. In other words, it is essential to the fiber and fabric of our lives.

As applied to business of all kinds, networking is a "must-do" strategy. It empowers, creates achievement, and unifies common organizational fields.

Nowadays, when we hear the word "networking", we don't think about community networking, but about computer networks. Networked computers are supposed to make our lives easier at home and work because they are speaking to each other.

However, computer networks don't speak to the power of community networks. Networking means building partnerships and alliances that help businesses expand their reach. There are compelling reasons to network.

You can exponentially increase your capacity to get money, services, and people buying your products. And you can have partners that offer their services or products at your business.

Networking works with outreach, as they are both about connecting with people. There is a socialization factor to both networking and outreaching that makes this process enjoyable. The ultimate goal of these approaches is to build relationships that benefit an organization and the people it serves.

The Bay Elementary School N Link

I don't know what would have happened if I hadn't had a successful partnership with the Bay Elementary School N. In the early days, we only had about $20,000 for each year of the initial three-year grant cycle from the state to provide stakeholder programs. We were lucky because the school's Healthy Start program manager got permission from her grant advisor to give us money we needed.

The Bay School's personnel aided us in forming supportive connections that led to tangible benefits. These included links to the local supervisors to community foundations for more grant money, which helped fund the center's first renovation and after-school programs.

Networking can also apply to networks of professionals working together to:

- Share vital information (as appropriate)
- Collectively solve problems
- Make money
- Instill important values
- Advocate at the corporate, city, state, or national level for companies that carry out specific work
- Share preferred practices
- Establish standards for your field
- Set policy
- Work together for the common good of the organizations involved

- Networking can pay substantial dividends

  Add your favorite activities to this list.

Cast a wide net

Not long after I started the center, I learned about a national center for family centers in Chicago that offered a large conference every other year. I attended four of their conferences over eight years.

One year I was able to take a team of three senior managers with me. It was exciting because it was an advantageous place to learn about and incubate new ideas, especially with a team present.

As a member of a citywide network (as I was), you can create strategies to achieve collective goals. These associations are wonderful resources for growing connections, selling products, and aiding community development.

Suggestions for networking

- Be an expert and present at a local conference and talk to people, get business cards, and follow up on appropriate potentials for partnerships.
- Attend national, regional, and/or citywide conferences and form new links with like-minded people.
- Have a table at local events with your literature and talk to other exhibitors or participants. It's a great place to find out about resources.
- Join and become involved in local business networks, particularly those in your field. Share information. See how you can help other organizations or vice versa.
- Become an expert in the topic of your calling. Let people come to you.

- Network with neighbors, friends, and family about specific concerns, needs, issues, and so on. You never know what might come out of these conversations.
- If you have government or other funder meetings, plan to network. This is a particularly helpful approach if you have an unmet service or financial need.
- Be a social influencer, use LinkedIn, Facebook, Instagram, Twitter, MeWe, Slack, and so on, to connect to your networks.
- Add your actions or those you want to try on this list for networking.

An amazing collaboration

In 1996, our partner, the Bay Elementary School N, applied for a Junior League family support grant. It was a new field in giving for the League. The Junior League, Inc. (JL), founded in 1901, is an educational women's volunteer organization aimed at improving communities and the social, cultural, and political fabric of society.

While the school received interest in its proposal, it was the organization I founded (mentioned in their application) that they were most responsive to. The main reason seemed to be that we were already aligned with the family center viewpoint, and the school is, well, a school.

Starting in 1997 and ending in 2004, we procured a $45,000 grant and had approximately twelve to fifteen volunteers a year during the seven years the JL was a funder.

Highlights of this teamwork

- We learned from the ground up how to implement a management program for the volunteers who ran a homework help program and the once-a-week child-oriented activity center.

- League volunteers created many positive networking opportunities for us.
- We were able to show other funders a successful, long-term working partnership that was giving us volunteers and grant income.
- We learned how to run effective, successful raffles.
- We acquired a first-rate board of director chair who held that position for fifteen years.

JL Story Continued

Most of the young women who volunteered with us during the Junior League grant period were employed by large national, if not international, corporations, such as Sega. I got a phone call one morning from one of my Junior League committee members who worked for Sega.

Camilla asked if I was interested in receiving some Sega video games for the center. I said of course, that we would be delighted and would take all they could send us. Camilla said she would see what was possible.

I thought we were talking about the handheld Sega Game Gears that were the rage at the time. Our kids attending our after-school program were crazy about these. I was overjoyed, believing that we would be able to give them out as gifts. A couple of months went by, and I forgot about this conversation.

One early afternoon in November, a gigantic truck pulled up in front of the center. I am not kidding; it was one of the longest trailer trucks I have ever seen. I had a small office with a window at the front of the building. I was going outside to scold the driver and ask him to move since he was blocking our entire pickup zone.

He explained that this was a delivery from Sega, and the packages had our address on them. I could feel my stomach drop. I thought to myself this was either thousands of Game Gears or something I wasn't expecting. My second guess was correct.

I believe there were close to FORTY massive, secondhand computer stations that had been display centers in stores. I remember being speechless for a few minutes as the trucker started to unload them one by one. They were all boxed up, so we were able to stack them in our hallway three on top of each other, two deep.

Our operations guy, Rex, and I looked at each other. He knew I was going to either laugh or cry. I decided it was ludicrous enough that I started to laugh and couldn't stop.

A couple of days later, Rex got on the phone with a slew of our nonprofit partners and told them what we had to offer. But first he went meticulously through every huge box and test-drove each computer to make sure it was fully operational. We kept five computer stations for our center. Five or six didn't work, but the rest were given away to other nonprofits serving families and children.

The best part of the story was that the kids treasured them and all of their functionalities. And I learned how to better communicate with all the center's funders, especially my Junior League associates, regarding donations.

I loved this collaboration and was genuinely sad when it ended. The Junior League said that it had been a fruitful partnership, and it was one of the longest associations they had ever had with a nonprofit organization.

It taught me the incredible value of networking, outreach, and open communications. This relationship with the Junior League was special because the partnership worked so well. I learned a lot about volunteers, funding, and the importance of expressing appreciation and encouragement.

Networking is exciting because it can take on a myriad of forms. Networks themselves often cater to a particular group or a grouping of specific services that share the same mission or purpose.

A list of local networks might include a community health network, a young professionals network, an entrepreneurs and investors network, and a social networking group, plus many more.

A group that comes together for the common good of a collective mission can be a powerful action-oriented alliance. Some of these groups specialize in advocacy as a collective, which, again, can prove to be very fruitful.

Understanding networking through outreach

Fill in the blanks:

1. The purpose of networking is______________________

   Answer: The purpose of networking is to find professionals who share your vision, mission, values and services or goods. They can offer your organization adjunct programs or products, a way to get funding (if needed), or an opportunity to come to the collective table to make something beneficial happen for your work.

2. The purpose of outreach is__________________________

   Answer: The purpose of outreach is to allow the information about your programs to be disseminated, so you have an appropriate turnout at your events and engagements.

3. The difference between networking and outreach is ________

   ____

   Answer: The difference between networking and outreach is that they each have different end goals and separate audiences in mind.

4. Business uses outreach and networking but adds another element, which is__________________________________

   Answer: Business uses outreach and networking but adds advertising. They can often spend multiple millions of dollars on a single campaign.

5. Networking, and outreach are great for building____

   Answer: Networking and outreach are great for building relationships and informally socializing. Connections are the very reason to enjoy outreach and networking because they can make advantageous things happen.

Both strategies are effective ways to see how deep and wide you and the impact of others can go, especially when you team up to make something happen.

The best part of either strategy is it assists the people you are reaching out to. It's best to use both since they have somewhat different audiences and purposes.

Networking demonstrates the importance of connecting with other businesses, funders, and individual donors; getting new sales leads; and finding potential board members. This can strengthen your ability to provide the necessary service/product components.

All this leads us to the importance of making time for those critical connections. They can make or break your ability to sell things or provide programs and services to the people you are trying to reach.

Whatever the circumstances, it takes going to where others are gathering (conferences, charitable speaking opportunities, conventions, tabling events, association meetings, etc.) and then sharing information. Networking and outreach are involved with building essential relationships.

Healthier by accident

A notable example of effective outreach and networking occurred in 2009 when the "swine flu" pandemic hit. The center was unprepared for the backlash from participants that we experienced. The service community was about 60 to 70 percent Asian (depending on the year) and approximately 25 percent Hispanic, with the rest a mix of other ethnicities.

I had just finished reading a comprehensive article in *TIME* magazine that mentioned how the virus had gone around the world, picking up steam as it went.

A blame game had erupted around this particular flu at the center I ran. Each ethnicity was blaming the other for the root cause. Many of our Asian participants donned masks and didn't want to mingle outside of their families. Attendance dropped steeply at all of the programs.

It was so bad that almost no one was attending classes or services. It was very dramatic. However, it was a clear opportunity to provide education on the participant level.

Additionally, the opportunity was ripe to network with other health care providers in the Bay Area. Simultaneously, because of effective networking, we had the chance to apply for a substantial health grant from a local foundation that specialized in health-related matters. Fortunately, we received the funding.

Because we had the money, we were able to expand our child-centered, health-related services and add the adult health programming that we always needed.

We had relationships with a few of the local hospitals and a department of public health. However, we expanded our partnerships through networking to encompass more health care providers. These health programs touched on all the services we offered that genuinely benefited our community. It worked out better in the long run for our participants than anyone could imagine.

Engaging networks

In the twenty-five years I had directed services at a nonprofit, I had been part of two successful iterations of family center networks in the Bay Area. A volunteer foundation funded the original family network in approximately 1996. There were seven or eight of us at the table during the three years the network was in existence.

The foundation that funded this original family center network paid for a very part-time facilitator who put together a data fact sheet with the family centers' input. Foundations and government officials locally received these fact sheets.

We learned that family centers were located throughout the Bay Area and offered households a combination of services. In 2000, money came from the state to all counties to fund family centers in a myriad of forms. These funds set up a government office to disseminate this money in the form of grants. A network is a great way to show a unified front in asking for more dollars from a governmental body.

The nonprofit I ran received funds from the grant. I mention this because it was one of the driving forces in funding and starting the second iteration of a family center network. We felt the field needed alliances, standards, advocacy, and training. We also wanted family-centered nonprofits to share their service expertise and personal best practices.

I was chair of their evaluation committee for seven years. During my tenure, the evaluation team created the first set of standards of family centers. Shortly after, they were mandated to be used by family centers by a government funder.

Some years later, the family center network merged them with "protective factors." These standards promoted child well-being. (See the Protective Factors website information at the end of this chapter.)

Think about networking

- On a scale of 1–5 (with 5 being the highest), how well does networking work for your organization? Why did you give it the rating you did?
- How have you used networking to get more money or publicity for your organization?
- What do you see as the value of networking?
- What skills might you acquire to become an expert networker?
- What local networks might you get involved in? Or why are you involved in a community network?

Think about each of these questions and the ramifications they have for your organization.

Networking is focused on sharing knowledge, resources, contacts, and advice with other professionals. It can offer additional perspective to your work. This is another way that people find out about what you do. Networking is so commonplace these days that we can't live without it.

In a for-profit business context, networking is used to socialize with others in business circles for multiple purposes. Email and social media have made it easy, both to share information and learn about in-person events where you can connect with others. Finding out how to do something better or connecting with others in the field are a few excellent reasons to network.

Networking can generate significant contacts if you join professional organizations. These associations stand to offer your organization vital programs or services, sales leads (for-profits), funding links (nonprofits), and other innumerable benefits.

For-profit networking ideas to put into practice

- Participate in business seminars, join professional associations, attend appropriate conferences and/or business luncheons, and so on. to meet and exchange ideas with others.
- Become a "social influencer" and be adept at posting marketing strategies or tips on a blog or other social media platforms.
- What you put out there about the company and yourself matters. Have integrity and honesty about what you do and say.

Nonprofit networking opportunities

- Build network associations to maximize business potentials.
- Networking has the potential to offer linkages to funding, relevant advocacy, improved services, or additional programming.
- You, too, can become a "social influencer" by using blogging or the many types of social media available.

More research on networking

- "What Is Business Networking, Definition and Examples of Business Networking," Susan Ward, The Balance: Small Business, https://www.thebalancesmb.com/what-is-business-networking-and-what-are-the-benefits-2947183
- "Nonprofit Networking: The New Way to Grow," Martha Lagace, *Working Knowledge*, May 2015, Harvard Business School, https://hbswk.hbs.edu/item/nonprofit-networking-the-new-way-to-grow

- "The Protective Factors Framework," Center for the Study of Social Policy: Strengthening Families, https://www.flgov.com/wp-content/uploads/childadvocacy/strengthening_families_protective_factors.pdf.

Books

- *The Art of Community: Seven Principles for Belonging*, Charles H. Vogl. Berrett-Koehler Publishers (2016).
- *The Well-Connected Community: A Networking Approach to Community Development, 3rd Edition*, Alison Gilchrist. Policy Press (2019).
- *Brand Storytelling: Put Customers at the Heart of Your Brand Story*, Miri Rodriguez. Kogan Page (2020).
- *Business Networking for Dummies*, Stefan Thomas. John Wiley & Sons (2014).

Chapter 9:
LONGEVITY
Sustainability

"Sustainability is not a goal to be reached, but a way of thinking, a way of being, a principle we must be guided by."

Giulio Bonazzi, Chairman, Aqualfil Group

Sustainability: *Able to last or continue for a long time.*

Merriam-Webster Learner's Dictionary

As Marilyn L. Donnellan wrote in *The Top Twenty Sustainability Strategies for Nonprofits,* "True sustainability is about building solid infrastructure and a culture of innovation, creativity, and growth." (See end of chapter for resources.)

It is an awesome feeling to look back twenty-five years and realize your business continues to be a success. This chapter offers guidance on how to build sustainability. It is an indispensable concept to cultivating a thriving, long-term establishment.

While the evidence and stories herein are (mostly) from a nonprofit perspective, many of these concepts can be adjusted for a moneymaking business lens. Sustainability, then, means that business can benefit from and stand the test of time. It can provide agility, staying power, and have enough funds and other right ingredients to endure adversities. Sustainability is the quality of being aware and protective of an organization's resources, especially the infrastructure (and all that includes).

Sustainability is a business approach to creating long-term value by taking into consideration how a given organization operates in the ecological, social, and economic environment. – *Why All Businesses Should Embrace Sustainability,* Professor Knut Haanaes, imd.org (See end of chapter for more resources.)

In an organizational context, sustainability includes the ever-critical financial support but encompasses more than just money. Other assets related to this concept might include the company's values, staff, working space, marketing, and technology. These ingredients of sustainability are necessary to accomplish business goals and carry out key activities.

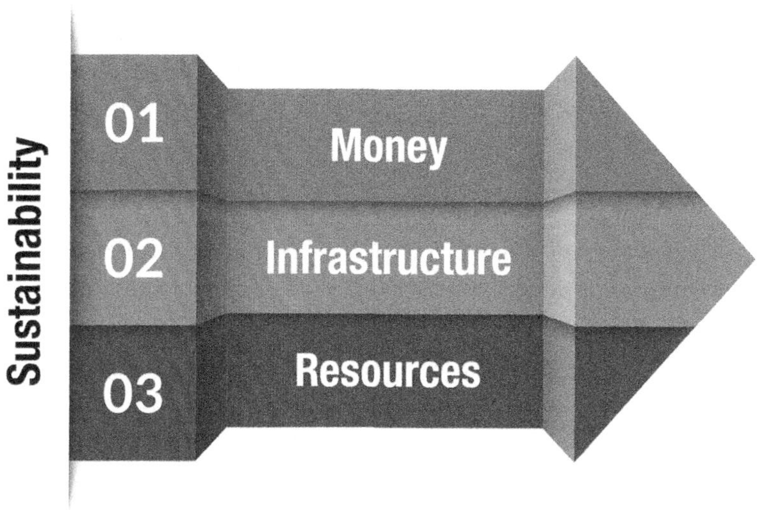

Sustainability allows business to be supple enough to endure setbacks and obstacles. It is a type of organizational resiliency (see Chapter 20 for more on this).

Sustainability is a business principle. Nonprofits are a business but are not necessarily seen through that lens. A basic paradigm shift is to treat nonprofits as the business they are. Sustainability is a central idea and mindset in running any organization, including charitable organizations.

Nonprofit finances are not always well secured in advance, making them more vulnerable to a downturn in giving or in the economy. It's imperative to create a robust infrastructure with strong finances that keeps the organization going for years to come.

While sustainability may make sense as an essential business concept, the application can be vague. If we are implementing sustainability at an organization, what does that mean and look like? Sustainability refers to the endurance and flexibility of an organization. It points to what needs to be in place for this to occur.

The components of sustainability often depend on the business but might contain the elements referenced above. Additionally, sustainability can involve evaluation, annual fundraising or money-making plans, financial management, training, strategic thinking, IT capacity, the board, and more. It enhances the ability to execute the mission of the business.

Being sustainable means we can respond to internal and external uncertainties as needed. The economy, demographics, politics, culture, and technology are in continuous fluctuation. Organizations must be agile enough to make the necessary changes required to stay relevant. Especially in these unsettled times.

Think about long-term sustainability:

- What strategies for sustainability do you currently utilize?
- How can values help to establish sustainability?
- What are the existing challenges facing the organization related to sustainability?
- Which ingredients could one use to grow the business toward longevity?
- Briefly, what can you set in motion to ensure sustainability now?
- If your organization is sound right now, what about five or ten years from now?
- What elements of sustainability would be helpful to have in place?\

Organizational sustainability formulas and templates can be found online or in books about business. As you have probably gathered, sustainability has a focus on the health of the organization including an emphasis on finances. It can also aid the organization in becoming more resilient (bouncing back after adversity).

What is organizational viability?

We can understand this concept by posing some scenarios. These situations might include: how does the organization handle leadership changes or a pandemic (like the COVID-19 virus) where everything shuts down? How do you stay relevant when there are a multitude of problems? Being sustainable means having plans for unforeseen events (the "what-ifs") and growing the business to reach its potential.

Strategies for potential organizational sustainability

- The organization has values that are embedded in the culture.
- Technology is up-to-date, possibly even cutting edge.
- The organization has operating reserves, or "rainy day funds."
- The mission statement of the business can function as a strong driving force.
- Outreach and networking are ongoing (Marketing 101) so as to build those indispensable relationships.
- The organization regularly manages, evaluates, and respects its resources.
- The organization has outcome measures for all of its programs, services, and/or products.
- Employees are respected and seen as the backbone of the organization. The infrastructure can withstand difficult situations since you have backup plans ready.
- Substantial strategies are in place that regularly bring in the funds.
- The people served have ways of making needs and requests known and applied (e.g., participant-requested services).

Bonus: You own your building.

Crazy good opportunity

A notable sustainability event opened up, seemingly out of the blue, just seven years after the center began. I had what most would consider a difficult landlord, whom I will call Sam.

At the time, he was in his mid-to-late sixties and drove a big red truck. He preferred to work with the part-time accountant (who was a man) rather than answer to me, a woman (who was in charge). It was a complicated relationship.

However, Sam was thrilled that we received government funding, since it was a dependable income. It enabled Sam to collect his rent on time each month. In late 1999, I noticed some businessmen "hanging out" in the front lobby, apparently sizing up the building. I thought, "Oh no, he's selling the building." I tracked him down.

I said, "Sam, are you putting the building up for sale?" He hedged a bit and answered, "I'm thinking about it." I told him we had wanted to buy the building all along if it ever came on the market.

He said, "Oh, okay, I will send you a brochure." I am not sure how he got so quickly from "thinking" about selling the building to selling the building with color brochures, but I immediately flew into action.

A young woman named June from a facility nonprofit had come in a year or so before and told me that if I ever wanted to buy the building, she might be able to help. At the time, I remember doing an internal eyeball roll and thinking, "Sure, whatever."

It turned out June ran an office out of a larger nonprofit. Her job was helping organizations with childcare services renovate or buy their building. Even though we had existed for less than eight years, we had already made numerous renovations to our space.

The idea of having to move seemed crazy. The reasons to avoid relocating were clear. Besides the countless remodels, the community had come to identify the nonprofit in that location as the place to go for child and family-centered services.

Also, owning real estate in the Bay Area is legendarily challenging because it can be so expensive. I called June and told her that our landlord already put the building on the market and asked if she could help.

June not only assisted us, but made it happen. We acquired another 2,500 square feet next door that had been parceled out to another tenant, and we subsequently refurbished that space.

Our board chair, our part-time finance person, and I closed on the building in early May 2000. It seemed like it was almost an unheard-of victory, but it happened, nonetheless.

I approached sustainability in a myriad of ways. Two distinct methods stand out:

1. We bought two (relatively) affordable buildings in fifteen years.
2. We had earned income streams through fees for our child-centered services and apartment rentals upstairs in the first building we bought.

Buying buildings as part of a sustainability strategy worked out better than I could have imagined. Having property created solid ground on which sustainability could grow.

The purchase made a strong statement to participants that we were grounded in the neighborhood and here to stay. I realize that in many areas of the country, this may not be possible or desired. However, it worked for us to anchor the nonprofit in the community.

Earned income was the second winning strategy I used for sustainability. We had two unrestricted or earned income streams. One came from program fees and the other came from our second-floor apartments.

Earned income rapidly became an essential part of our revenue stream, as it was unrestricted dollars. In other words, you are allowed to use the money as you see fit. I continued to fundraise and subsidize the fee-based programs since we weren't charging participants the market rate.

Infrastructure components

The infrastructure components that the *Stanford Social Innovation Review* includes in its list are:

- Sturdy information technology systems
- Strong financial systems
- Skills training
- Fundraising processes

The *Stanford Social Innovation Review* notes, "Organizations that build robust infrastructure have a much higher chance of staying around" (ssir.org).

A research organization called the Batten Group sees "7 key drivers of sustainability in nonprofits." Their list contains these essential items:

1. Money
2. Mission
3. A dedicated team
4. An engaged board
5. Leadership and succession planning
6. Program capacity
7. Financial understanding of costs and overhead

Source: Blog post on "7 Key Drivers of Sustainability," https://thebattengroup.com/7-key-drivers-of-sustainability-in-non-profits/

How to master sustainability is food for thought. I agree with both the *Stanford Innovation Review* and the Batten Group. Additionally, sustainability is a synergy of all of the elements we have been talking about.

It creates a level of endurance that organizations need. The lists that talk about how to build a robust infrastructure are helpful applications. Also, there is a certain amount of serendipity and luck that establishes sustainability.

Yay for earned income

Seeking funding in 1995–96, I called the foundations I had heard of, a pretty good list of 8 to 10 organizations. Although people answered their phones in those days, I got the cold shoulder. Foundation staff said to call back when we had "established" ourselves. Of course, this was a "catch-22" since we needed money to offer our community programs and develop the center. These same foundation folks couldn't figure out which neighborhood our site was located in.

I realized I had a small window of time to offer participant-requested services to the community. I wanted to make sure I met stakeholder needs, grew trust, and established a team that would aide me in shaping the center. Through surveys and focus groups, people had already made known what they desired. At stake was keeping community members' interest and the fledgling nonprofit's credibility intact.

The finance/admin guy, (Rex) saw my dilemma but said, "If you want to offer these programs to the community soon, you have little choice but to charge fees so you can staff them professionally. Foundations aren't going to help at this point."

I had sworn to myself that any programs we were going to offer to this low-income, diverse community would have to be free. After some genuine hand-wringing, I decided to provide quality early childhood education and after-school programs for low fees.

We started with a sliding scale, but it quickly became too much work for our minimal administrative staff of one part-time person. Also, participants rapidly figured out workaround(s).

For example, a family of four was only showing an income of $13,000, yet they also received money from abroad, and mom ran a cash seamstress business out of her home. We had more than a few instances.

Since we had to move quickly, we scratched the sliding scale and went with a flat rate for both programs with a service exchange for people who couldn't afford the programs.

The service exchange offered families an opportunity to trade their skills for program fees for their children. We launched and filled both programs to very appreciative audiences.

We had three distinct benefits:

1. Earned income is an effective development strategy, as funds can be applied where needed. This includes administrative positions and other areas funders historically won't pay for.
2. Participants are okay about paying nominal fees for programs because they believe paid services offer distinctly more value than free ones.
3. We learned how to be sustainable.

Fund balance

When you speak of sustainability, you need to have enough money. The infrastructure can withstand difficult situations since you have backup financial plans ready. That is why it is essential to mention the significance of creating a fund balance or a rainy-day fund. It is a best practice for any business. It can address sustainability, as well as development issues.

It is absolutely true that every business needs to have adequate cash balances available to support the timing of payroll and other expenses, as well as to pay for unanticipated costs or increases. It's a myth, however, that a single standard applies for all nonprofits. From "Operating Reserves for Nonprofits," Kate Barr, National Council of Nonprofits, councilofnonprofits.org. (See end of chapter for resources.)

Substantial strategies are in place that regularly bring in the funds. However, establishing a fund balance is easier said than done. Depending on what's going on with an organization at any given time, it can be next to impossible. Nonprofit culture, particularly with small nonprofits under a million dollars, unfortunately seems to be "hand-to-mouth." Regular operating fundraising is a challenge, let alone raising money for a reserve fund.

Creating set-aside money can be a problem for any size organization, especially if you follow industry standards of keeping three months of operating expenses on hand. Boards, including others that may be "in charge" of an organization, need to understand it's not usually negligence that stops a business from having a fund balance. It's most often competing priorities.

In twenty-five years, the only time I pushed back on having a fund balance was when I was fundraising for a renovation for our branch office that cost over $2 million. Simultaneously, I was raising money to meet the annual organizational budget. The board was pressuring me to grow our set-aside money.

We had a small fund balance at the time, equaling about a month's worth of operating. Money was tight, and I was worried about making the annual budget. While I understood board concerns, it was unfeasible to grow the fund balance, so I couldn't do it. If, however, one accomplishes a fund balance, it offers security for uncertain times. This is true for every operating business.

Sustainability is an important approach to practice no matter what sector you are in. Sound financial management is key to business longevity. But it's just one piece of the puzzle. Sustainability helps to protect the overall organization's resources and gain the responsiveness to do so. It's like having an additional insurance policy for your business. It enhances your ability to strategically expand your infrastructure, ensuring long-term continuity.

Think about sustainability

- What does sustainability mean to you?
- What does a vital infrastructure entail?
- Do you have enough money to meet the growth needs of the company?
- Why do you think technology and marketing are essential infrastructure components?
- Where do you think values fit into the concept of sustainability?
- Do you use any earned income strategies? Why or why not?
- Do you have a fund balance? If so, how is your business growing it or spending it down?
- How are resource development and sustainability handled now at your organization? How would you prefer them to be handled?

The sooner you begin to view business through the sustainability lens, the better. Sustainability can build a strong infrastructure that in turn can withstand the setbacks at any given time. This is a for-profit business strategy that can significantly advance a nonprofit's mission. There are only token excuses left for a business not embarking on sustainability planning.

Sustainability is a powerful solution for vital infrastructure advancement. Because infrastructure has numerous components, make sure to be honest and select portions of the business that need the most work. Remember that good sustainability is the "wheels on the bus" that can move you to longevity.

For-profit sustainability ideas to put into practice

- A sustainability lens can help you manage and evaluate resources, which can lead to better profits, improved quality, and lower overhead.
- Be proactive: Use risk management tools regularly to determine where the sustainability issues lie. Smooth out bumps instead of being surprised by the challenges they create.

Nonprofit sustainability opportunities

- Become proficient at knowing when and where to plug in a company's resources.
- Exercise transparency to build open communication within the work environment
- Focus on the infrastructure of the organization. Assess where you are. Take the appropriate steps to know if you need to expand, cut back, or hold the line.

More Research on Sustainability

- "9 Strategies All Startups Must Have to Sustain Business Growth," Startup Grind, https://www.startupgrind.com/blog/9-strategies-all-startups-must-have-to-sustain-business-growth/
- "The Secret to Sustainability for Nonprofit Organizations," Ann Latham, Forbes.com, March 2016, https://www.forbes.com/sites/annlatham/2016/03/27/the-secret-to-sustainability-for-non-profit-organizations/?sh=640a584e6abe

- "Creating Long-Term Nonprofit Sustainability," Eric Burger, VolunteerHub.com, https://www.volunteerhub.com/blog/long-term-nonprofit-sustainability/
- "Nonprofit Sustainability: Preparing for Growth," Madeleine Monson-Rosen, MissionBox Global Network, June 2019, https://www.missionbox.com/article/50/nonprofit-sustainability-preparing-for-growth
- "Why All Businesses Should Embrace Sustainability," Knut Haanaes, IMD—International Institute for Management Development, November 2016, https://www.imd.org/research-knowledge/articles/why-all-businesses-should-embrace-sustainability/
- "A Guide to Organizational Resources and How to Manage Them," Grantham University, May 2019, https://www.grantham.edu/blog/a-guide-to-organizational-resources-and-how-to-manage-them/
- "Nonprofit Sustainability," Operating Reserves for Nonprofits," Kate Barr, National Council of Nonprofits, https://www.councilofnonprofits.org/tools-resources/nonprofit-sustainability

Books

- *The Top Twenty Sustainability Strategies for Nonprofits: Techniques to Ensure Long-Term Growth and Sustainability,* Marilyn L. Donnellan. CreateSpace (2018).
- *Nonprofit Sustainability: Making Strategic Decisions for Financial Viability*, Jeanne Bell, Jan Masaoka, and Steve Zimmerman. Jossey-Bass (2010).
- *7 Nonprofit Income Streams: Open the Floodgates to Sustainability,* Karen Eber Davis. CharityChannel Press (2014).

Author's Note: Many of the websites and for-profit books on sustainability have to do with the environment.

Chapter 10:
MULTIPLYING MONEY!
Development

"The ultimate resource in economic development is people, not capital or raw material that develops an economy."

Peter Drucker, business expert and author

Business Development: *Companies seek sources of funding to grow the business. Funding represents an act of contributing resources to finance a program, product, project or need.*

From "What Are Sources of Funding?" corporatefinanceinstitute.com

Nonprofit Development: *Nonprofit development is to raise funds for the company's various philanthropic efforts. These efforts can include just about any community or humanitarian initiative that provides people in the community with a service or fills a need.*

smallbusiness.chron.com

Resource development is the process of assessing existing assets and the ability to grow them. Fundraising is focused on seeking financial support. These are crucial ways for most businesses to bring in revenue and other benefits for their organization.

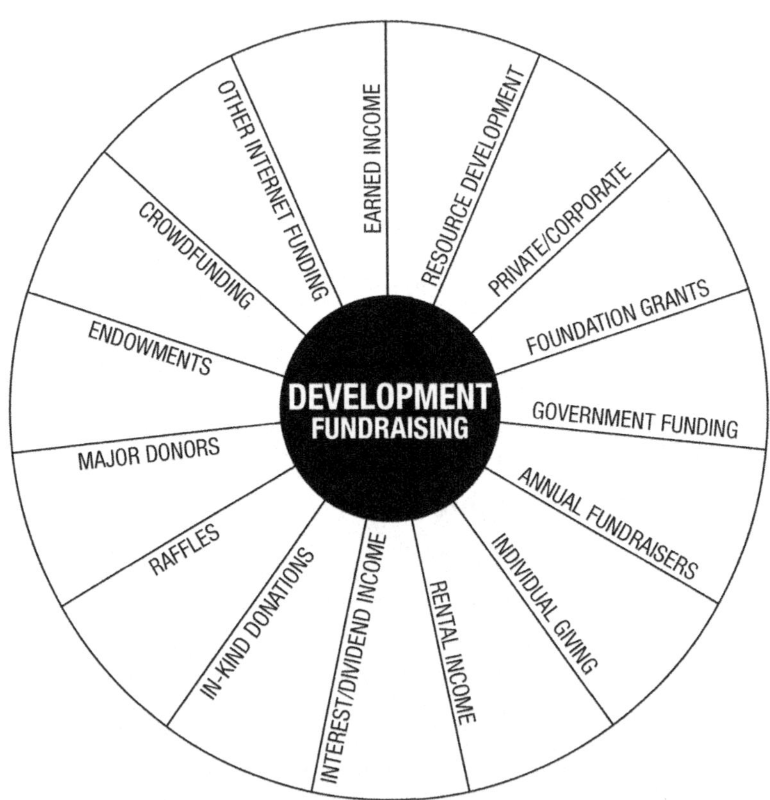

What's in a label—development, fundraising, or both?

This specific issue of whether to call it development or fundraising pertains to nonprofits and large educational institutions (e.g., colleges and universities). However, labeling uncertainties can get confusing for any type of business.

So, which is it? Fundraising, development, or could it be a hybrid? What is the function called that raises money for an organization? Fundraising and development are used interchangeably to imply the same thing. However, I'll give it a unique twist and say that fundraising operates as a subcategory of development.

I have found that the terminology for both changes depending on the size of the organization and what the business prefers. The more research I do on development and fundraising, the more I am convinced that there is only a small consensus on what the words signify and how they are applied. Everyone agrees that while the terms are similar, they might not represent the same thing.

Development has come to mean the larger component that encompasses fundraising. It integrates all of the aspects of fundraising plus pays attention to resource development. However, fundraising best describes the nitty-gritty when it comes to raising money (e.g., writing applications for grants, online strategies, or annual fundraisers). Fundraising then functions as a grouping under development, and fundraising is often associated with nonprofits.

Large development departments at significant nonprofits, institutions, and colleges/universities probably disagree with these descriptions. Most of the development officers at these places cultivate individual donors as their primary development activity. These persons are there to secure endowments, estate planning, and significant gifts.

Please don't get hung up on definitions. Call it what you want, as long as it serves your purposes of raising money. We will use the word "development" to indicate all one does to secure capital and/or resources. Fundraising falls under the category of development and applies to the specific tools and techniques used to raise money.

Fundraising

While there is a difference in fundraising techniques between Corporate America and nonprofit organizations, the idea is to raise money. For-profit fundraising often happens when an organization is looking for investors to put their funds into the company so it can grow and have a bigger profit margin. Most charitable organizations must sustain their operating and program expenses by fundraising. So, while there are differences, there are ideas that each entity can learn from.

There's a popular song that says, "Love Makes the World Go Round." And there are those critics who disagree and say it's money. Like any business, a nonprofit needs enough funds to build capacity and infrastructure to meet its purpose or mission.

Any of the many online articles or books about fundraising will give you a particular number of steps to build a successful fundraising program. There are also numerous fundraising templates to get you started. What follows is common wisdom about fundraising and its necessary elements.

Effective fundraising considerations

- Build positive, genuine relationships with a potential funder or buyer. Establish a partnership whenever possible.
- Understand the funder (or purchaser) and the role it plays in your organization.
- One size doesn't fit all. Use an approach best suited to a potential donor/customer.
- Practice strategic thinking and apply it to potential methodologies.
- Never "chase" money. In other words, do not go after dollars that don't quite fit your constituents or your mission.

- Sell your organization's mission, purpose, and services (or products).
- Demonstrate through numbers, statistics, demographics, testimonials, and so on. that your organization is offering cost-effective solutions to problems your participants (or buyers) face.
- Describe concisely but systematically who your organization is and what it does.
- Make the case that the business you represent is competent financially and programmatically and can handle the proposed dollar amount.
- Create an annual fundraising plan. Include how much money you need to raise, what strategies you will use to get there, where you will get the anticipated funds, and when you expect to receive the money.

Fundraising and sales sing the perfect duet

Money is the goal of fundraising. And as mentioned earlier, when you execute fundraising, it is a sophisticated type of selling that involves your personal and organizational strengths and values. One of the most critical pieces to success in raising money is to handle fundraising like refined selling.

"Whatever your career goals or aspirations are, the 'art of sales' is a crucial skill to learn," Ryan Clements notes. "Every day we sell things in many different capacities. We sell our ideas and our products. We sell our values. We sell the causes that we care about." (See end of chapter for resources.) Notice how Clements mentions values. Everyone selling is promoting values, ideas, and causes to funders or customers. It is very relationship based. In the for-profit business environment, selling is based on our connections with others and hopefully is inclusive of ethical standards.

Clements says that highly successful salespeople know that effective selling techniques are about:

- Effective questioning
- Understanding the needs of another
- The ability to show empathy
- Being present
- Value-added solutions to problems

The next time you get the shudders when someone tells you he/she is going into sales, don't think of the slick, fast-talking, used car salesperson. Selling doesn't mean giving your soul away to make the deal. Keep your integrity intact. People in business, including nonprofits, *sell* their organizations.

Folks in nonprofits may not realize they are selling something, but they are. They are promoting the business, their case statement, their programs and services, and the participants they are helping. In other words, they are in fact *selling* their organizational values to prospective partners, foundations, and other funders.

Sales is about establishing yourself as a trustworthy representative of the business. Profitable selling is not just about a financial exchange, it's the demonstration of passionate beliefs in the values, products, or services you are selling. A constructive relationship plays an essential role in making the deal. It's about the genuine worth for the provider and the receiver. At its best, selling is a mutual deal with both parties winning.

If at first you don't succeed, try again

This story began after we bought our building in 2000. At that time, we were looking for ways to pay it off and renovate a portion of it. I spoke with Miles, a funder who specialized in family centers and capital campaigns. Miles agreed to consider giving us a substantial grant for the building by looking at our community served and our financials.

Miles asked us to organize an extravaganza of community members, participants, funders, staff, community partners, and board members to kick off a potential partnership with the funder. We agreed. Fortunately, he agreed to pay for lunch (out of foundation funds) for all the parties joining us.

We had close to two hundred people attend the ceremonies. Many of the community members we'd invited had speaking roles. At the end of it, we had a business meeting with the foundation officer, our accountant, the board chair, and me.

While we did substantial hoop-jumping to get the event organized and were prepared for the business meeting, Miles still didn't seem comfortable giving us foundation money. We threw up our hands and realized we just couldn't meet the funder's expectations at this time.

Two years flew by. We raised the needed capital from numerous funders for the renovation and opened a branch office in a nearby underserved neighborhood. By then, I had heard through the grapevine that Miles was disappointed that we hadn't contacted him again.

When we heard that Miles and the foundation were still interested in our programs, we decided to ask for a grant for our branch office. He seemed concerned that we would request a donation when we hadn't followed up with our last request. However, Miles said we could fill out a grant application for our satellite agency. After putting in considerable work on the proposal, we received a very generous contribution.

The story ends well because we received foundation money from them for almost a decade. While the funder could be a problematic taskmaster, Miles knew what he wanted. He taught us how to write a well-crafted grant application by reworking the proposals multiple times.

When our time with the foundation was nearing an end, Miles asked if we were serious about buying a building for the branch that the foundation had continuously funded. I said we were. I pounded the neighborhood's pavement for two years until I found the perfect spot to renovate and move into.

I excitedly called Miles. And months later, when we were closing on the building, the foundation gave us a considerable donation, way more than they originally pledged. I was speechless. The best part for me was that Miles said they increased the donation amount because of my genuine dedication to the families served.

This account is about the power of relationships, values, and funding, even if it requires patience to make happen. Remember the importance of these partnerships, whether you seek money from individual donors, foundations, or corporations.

Show funders what you can offer by serving your constituents. Demonstrate to donors that they are investing in the organization's future and the ability to help the population served.

This approach shows values matter (trusting work relationships) and can add to the bottom line of making profits.

Social contagion

Development and fundraising emphasize the significance of sales and the relational nature of fundraising. This is the lifeblood of most nonprofits. Positive sales techniques are excellent relationship builders. It is an understatement to say people influence people. An example of this is something called social contagion.

This means that we are affected by someone else's actions. The contagion of kindness demonstrates that when we see someone else being nice, we almost instinctively feel that we could be doing the same thing. The behavior of others can be inspirational. This idea can work with for-profit business, too, since we are talking about human behavior.

Examples of the contagion of kindness are highly visible at in-person fundraisers for nonprofits. There is typically a time at fundraising events when people pledge money for a cause. A facilitator comes onstage and announces what the audience is potentially contributing to and how much is needed (e.g., money for a building wing, a new program, or a play structure).

The facilitator can start high or low, but a wonderful thing happens. I know from personal experience that I and others had little or no intention to contribute. Yet, we would suddenly find ourselves writing a check or giving a credit card number. This is the contagion of kindness in action. We are stimulated by others' generosity.

Create unique fundraising opportunities

Fundraising can take different forms. It's possible to get funds, sponsorship, or corporate support for any of the following: films, a dance party, playing team games, donor requests at a private home, bake sales, a recipe book, crowd funding, a fun run, endowments, and raffles (whatever will appeal to your audience).

This list might also include advocating for money from a foundation, a local government agency, or an individual donor. Think outside the box. Be creative and innovative, think differently, and be optimistic that it will work out.

Here are several ideas that might help raise funds.

- ***Assemble an annual development guide*** with financial benchmarks to follow for the year. Use a development manual to help with organizing your annual fundraising strategies. Be sure that it:

- is easily shared with others,
- contains approximate dates when each fundraising strategy will be completed,
- covers all "to be raised" revenues and their approaches, and
- assembles all the information in one slim handbook.

I highly recommend this strategy as an organized approach to development. The chief executive, the board, and development people get to see the same inclusive document. You can follow it regularly as it is updated and measure how you are doing. This is one place where it is beneficial to put "all your eggs in one basket."

Find a development handbook that works for your organization. Gather all your fundraising strategies for the year and organize them into categories. Assign a realistic financial value to them. Keep checking regularly to see how you are doing with your efforts. The handbook can be detailed if it is helpful.

A development guidebook creates an easy reminder of what the organization said it was going to do for any given year. Once you find the right template to track your annual funds, it's not as much work moving forward. You gain invaluable experience and perspective, so the next year, it becomes an even more relevant tool for the organization.

- ***Analyze the appropriate staffing for your development program.*** One factor to consider: As the executive director, are you the only one raising money for the organization? That might be a problem since your other crucial duties could take a back seat.

Think about these questions before you hire a development professional:

- How much can you afford to spend on a development expert, ideally and realistically? Does the organization want contract help (e.g., grant writer), part-time, full-time, or a whole team of specialists to divide up the functions?

- What would this person be hired to do?
- Pencil out a potential job description that would accurately portray their duties in the time they've been given.
- Decide if there are any specific skills this person(s) should possess, such as approaching individual donors, planning and running fundraising events, or developing marketing materials.
- Hire an individual who has relational abilities with funders. Additionally, they need to possess commitment, passion, and knowledge of the mission of the organization.
- If you are considering hiring someone for general development, what are they good at and what does the organization really need?

Diversified funding

A for-profit company might think of diversification as having someone who oversees several lines of unrelated business products or services. Diversified funding for a nonprofit is a concept that is akin to this but not quite the same.

Maybe you are new to development or wondering what diversified funding signifies for a nonprofit. A simple definition is not getting the entire annual income from one source. For instance, if all your dollars come from individual donors or from the government (for various reasons), you will be more at risk of losing your income than you would be if it came from various funding sources.

The topic of diversified funding comes up regularly, especially in master's programs for nonprofit management. To academia and others, diversified funding means (I am asking you to pretend here) dividing your approximate allocation of funding among each of these three entities: government, corporations, and individuals (with 10 perccent left to figure out). Some consider this the ideal spread of diversified money.

I took a workshop from a respected consultant who has been in the field of nonprofits for over thirty years. She advised us to forget the 30-30-30 distribution in the textbooks. It's hard work to fund nonprofits. Concentrate on getting the money needed for your organization, regardless of its source.

However, governments and foundations change their funding priorities with some regularity. It's smart sustainability planning to consider how you would fill the gap if this money went away. This is where having funding diversity makes sense.

If you don't ask, you don't get

Four years after its founding, the center had doubled the number of people served. This was thanks to the addition of a children's playgroup, an after-school program, a parent advisory board, and an early childhood education program (culled from participant-driven services techniques).

Covertly doubling the number of participants can be unspoken nonprofit code for needing more money. We were successfully helping families in the neighborhood by providing high-quality services, driven by their requests.

I applied for a city grant that had earmarked money for nonprofits. I received the same allocation that we got the previous year, even though our grant application demonstrated that our services had doubled. That response to the grant request was disappointing, to say the least.

At approximately the same time, I heard about a short meeting with the mayor that took place every other month on a Saturday, starting first thing in the morning. And it was, as you can imagine, competitive.

The mayor's office had a brilliant strategy: Give out tickets at 4.00 a.m. weeks in advance until they were gone. They went very quickly because there were only two dozen of them. We had explicit instructions from a city official on how to maximize the short time we would have to make our case to the mayor. You could talk about any municipal topic but had to keep it to ten minutes, including questions and answers.

On the appointed day in May, I took a group (including the finance person and a few parents) to the room where the presentations were held. The mayor had assembled a formidable team of department heads of at least a dozen strong. He walked in about eight minutes late and appeared annoyed.

Since it was before the days of PowerPoint, I had painstakingly put together a cut-and-paste presentation on butcher-block paper. It was a concise, written display for the mayor and his staff to view in bold, readable print. The report included the changing demographics in this family-friendly neighborhood.

I felt like I had succeeded in making a strong case for getting help with the funding shortfall. The first thing the mayor did was close his eyes while I set up the easel with the presentation. I was concerned since it contained vital information for making my case. Also, I had spent the better part of a week putting it together.

However, I could tell the mayor was engaged. When I finished, he pounded his fist on the table and said, "Why wasn't this woman's agency funded?" Viola, who oversaw the allocation of monies to the grantees as the acting department head, attended this meeting. She decided to answer the mayor by debating with him about why we didn't get increased dollars.

That was a significant mistake. He contradicted Viola and was dismissive of her. The mayor said it was unacceptable that I didn't receive the funding, as I made an excellent case for it. The tension in that conference room was palpable. I felt awful for Viola. The mayor then demanded his department heads find the $35,000 we were short.

On the way out of the meeting room, Viola whispered under her breath, "Thanks a lot, Maryann." While I was pleased to have been heard and promised more funding, I was worried about my relationship with Viola. She was a funder I had to continue to work with. In time, I was able to build a bridge with her. And, as promised, I received from the mayor's office the money that covered our shortfall.

Why do people give money to charities?

"In 2018 charitable giving was 410 billion dollars."

givingusa.org/giving

"55.5 percent of American households say that they give to charity."

psychologytoday.com

If you read about why people make donations to charitable organizations, you will find numerous reasons. However, it appears that there is common ground. Please refer to the list in the box as a summary of the common, compelling reasons why people contribute to causes. There are no surprises, but it makes for interesting study.

The most common reasons people donate

- Benefactors need a charity they trust and believe in their "good" work.
- People genuinely want to make a difference.
- Donors believe in a specific cause and wish to help.
- Personal stories from nonprofits motivate individuals.
- People use their good fortune to help others less fortunate.

- Giving is a family tradition.
- Prospective donors are cultivated and asked questions.
- The tax break at the end of the year is a great incentive.
- Religious giving is enormous and usually tops the scales each year. Tithing helped make religious giving famous.
- It "just feels good" or is "deeply rewarding."
- In the end, the reasons that people give are unique and individual.

Why do people no longer give or not give at all to nonprofits?

- Financial constraints.
- No one asked them.
- They gave their money to something or someone else.
- The charity had run amok, and donors no longer trusted it.
- "Because they stop thinking that they or their gift matter to your organization," according to Linda Lombardi, networkforgood.com/thenonprofitblog

This table is based on an online survey of 819 Americans, published in the *Nonprofit and Voluntary Sector Quarterly.*

Reasons to Give (rated on a scale of 1 to 5)		
1.	Altruism	4.21
2.	Trust	3.71
3.	Social	3.15
4.	Egoism	2.2
5.	Tax	2.06

The numbers in the table are the averages on a 1–5 scale, with 5 indicating that a reason is a significant motivation.

Source: "The Conversation," CC-BY-ND, Femida Handy and Sara Konrath, *Nonprofit and Voluntary Sector Quarterly*, November 2017.

It is important to remember why people give and why they don't. Folks need to be asked, but just as vital is that so many believe in altruism, which the dictionary defines as "an unselfish regard or devotion to the welfare of others." Donors have reported that altruism, as opposed to tax breaks, is at the top of their list of reasons for making donations to charitable causes.

No matter how intimidating fundraising can be, it is imperative to keep in mind that if people believe in a nonprofit's good work, they are happy to contribute.

Think about development/fundraising practices:

- What are the three primary sources of revenue at the organization of interest?
- How is this income cultivated in this business?
- What are your attitudes on "selling" the organization to donors for money? Can these get in the way of getting the gift?
- Do you use relational techniques for fundraising? How effective is this?
- How much time is spent on fundraising or how many development positions fundraise for your nonprofit or corporation on an annual basis? Is it enough?
- What do you understand about the concept of social contagion or social kindness? How do you apply it to the organization you are involved in?
- Which of the reasons that people give money to companies resonates the most for you?

- Which of the reasons that people stop giving to organizations resonates with you?
- From your own experience, what could you add to the pros and cons of why people give or don't give?

To summarize, "development" in the for-profit business arena is often referred to as "resource development," and "sales" is the term used to describe a version of fundraising. It is crucial for organizational sustainability because companies need money to function and expand the business. Without the necessary attention to development and the fundraising or selling that goes with it, most businesses wouldn't exist.

Development and fundraising are *relational* and sales oriented. There is no lack of fundraising or sales information out there on how to do it. No matter what business we are in, it's essential to have funds, but it can be a challenge. Asking people for money can be daunting, time-consuming, and frustrating. And the power imbalance in receiving money is real.

There's more than one great technique that will get you the grant or the sale. Have the right attitude, do your homework, gain sales expertise, think outside the box, use thoughtfulness, and speak to how an organization fits into the bigger picture. Sales and fundraising are most often a negotiation. It does take time. But in the end, when the needed funds are ensured, or we meet our goals, it can feel incredibly rewarding.

For-profit development and fundraising ideas to put into practice

- Development and fundraising most often equal revenue. Think outside the box, determine what resources you need, borrow ideas from the nonprofit field (if appropriate), and apply successful sales techniques to win more profits.

- Use values to sell more products and increase revenues.
- Customers can be motivated by how they feel about the company and how they perceive their business is making a difference in the world (e.g., values). Make sure your company is unrelenting about bettering the planet through the demonstration of your values.

Nonprofit development and fundraising opportunities

- Development staff need to relate well to others and gain those all-important funder relationships that lead to financial support.
- Fundraising delivers the crucial financial support you need to sustain your programs, products, or services.
- While fundraising is often the bread and butter for nonprofits, simultaneously, in the for-profit world, it is essential to "sell" the company's values and help the funder understand why their money matters.

More research on development and fundraising

- "Fundraising Basics for Nonprofits," The Balance: Small Business, https://www.thebalancesmb.com/fundraising-4161498
- "14 Corporate Fundraising Ideas: Proven to Get Your Employees to Give," Charity Auctions Today, https://www.charityauctionstoday.com/p/corporate-fundraising-ideas/
- "Nonprofit Fundraising 101: Honing Your Ask," Kelly Kulp, July 2018, https://wapix.co/nonprofit-fundraising-101-honing-your-ask/

- "Nonprofit Fundraising," Nolo, https://www.nolo.com/legal-encyclopedia/nonprofit-fundraising
- Effective Selling Techniques That Everyone Should Know and Use, Ryan Clements, https://www.ivyexec.com/career-advice/2015/effective-selling-techniques-that-everyone-should-know-and-use/
- "9 Tips for Effective Business Development," Bruna Martinuzzi, September 2015, https://www.americanexpress.com/en-us/business/trends-and-insights/articles/tips-effective-business-development/
- "The Most Successful 21+ Corporate Fundraising Ideas," Fundly blog, https://blog.fundly.com/corporate-fundraising-ideas/
- "5 Reasons Why People Give Their Money Away—Plus 1 Why They Don't," theconversation.com, https://theconversation.com/5-reasons-why-people-give-their-money-away-plus-1-why-they-dont-87801

Books

- *The Soul of Money: Reclaiming the Wealth of Our Inner Resources*, Lynne Twist. W.W. Norton & Company (2005).
- *Raise More Money from Your Business Community: The Workbook*, Linda Lysakowski. CharityChannel Press (2014).
- *Beyond Fundraising: New Strategies for Nonprofit Innovation and Investment*, Kay Sprinkle Grace. Wiley (2005).
- *The Generosity Network: New Transformational Tools for Successful Fund-Raising*, Jennifer McCrea and Jeffery C. Walker with Karl Weber. Deepak Chopra (2013).
- *The 1-Page Marketing Plan: Get New Customers, Make More Money, and Stand Out from the Crowd*, Allan Dib. Page Two (2018).

Chapter 11:
FINDING PURPOSE
Mission Statements

"My mission in life is not merely to survive, but to thrive."

Maya Angelou

Mission Statement: *A mission statement is a short sentence or paragraph that is used by a company to explain its purpose for being.*

Investopedia

My intention throughout this book is to always question the status quo. The ideas in these pages are deliberate. They are to make one think about how vital business concepts and humane principles are carried out. Mission statements give us a unique opportunity to do this.

You must have a mission for your organization. Furthermore, it has to make sense to employees and the people who participate in your services or buy your products. Mission statements can be a powerful declaration about the company's intention. A well-executed mission statement can open doors to success.

This chapter speaks to why it's critical to have a great mission statement. Additionally, it explains how to craft one that captures the essence of the business.

A strong mission statement defines the organization's intention, cause, and direction. It communicates the values a business can deliver, what groups it serves, and how. A mission statement helps prioritize what you can focus on and what you hope to change.

Easy steps to understand a mission statement

Step 1. It is *the* mission of the organization.

Step 2. The mission is captured in a concise, memorable statement.

Step 3. The mission statement reflects and encompasses the values and services of the business.

Step 4. Recognize that a mission statement can become an optimum marketing tool.

The mission statement is an internal and external device that naturally incorporates values. For example, it can shape organizational culture and can attract people who share the same principles. In turn, these persons can become employees, donors, buyers, volunteers, participants, and board members. Individuals, including benefactors, often choose an organization because of its mission.

A compelling mission statement can inspire people to act for the organization. Another essential quality of a noteworthy mission is that it's an outline for potential decision-making. To illustrate this point: Does the program, product, or service you're thinking of creating fall under your mission statement? Would it benefit your community based on how your mission statement describes it?

You can then imagine how the mission of the business can become a driving force. It gives direction when you are unsure. And it can provide an obvious way forward. It confirms that these decisions can serve your intended community. It's an excellent clarifier on focus, motivation, decision-making, and messaging to the public.

Most in the nonprofit and some in the business field are there to make a difference. One way a business can speak to this is with its mission statement. It can also remind many stakeholders of how your organization is different from others in the same field. We can become invested in the mission of a business, especially if it's persuasive, even if it does similar work as another organization.

However, if it were easy to create this kind of enlightened mission statement, then organizations might not have to work hard to convince others of their significant work. Yet, who better than you and your staff to create the perfect mission statement that frames your fundamental purposes to a T?

Ready, set, go! Create that awesome mission statement

Getting started on generating an effective mission statement is a significant yet time-consuming activity. And it can be daunting. The good news is that there are many websites and books that will take you step-by-step through this process.

The unique reason for the existence of your business is that you and/or your staff possess passion and excitement for the work you do. This very passion can take you to that great mission statement that captures what you do *better* than a professional writer might.

Give the formation of the mission statement some elbow grease and see what you can come up with. It doesn't have to be perfect or encompass all the descriptors below. However, it must represent your organization and what you are giving back to society.

The words below can apply to either a mission or vision statement.

A mission statement is a short general statement (ten to twenty words) that should be:

- Clear / Concise
- Memorable / Useful
- Short: Each word ideally will have meaning

- Inspiring / Keep it short
- Uncomplicated / Understandable
- Simple / Action Oriented
- Able to set a positive direction
- Able to explain the organization's existence
- A call to action
- Able to convey your purpose
- Able to communicate what you do

Think about crafting a new mission statement

- What is the purpose of the organization? Why does it exist?
- Who does it serve? Who is your target audience?
- How do you serve your constituents? What are the products, programs, and/or services?
- Can we accomplish this purpose? Is it in the realm of the possible or the near-impossible?
- What are your values?
- Is the organization local, national, or international?

Think about existing mission statements

- Does your current mission statement continue to represent your purpose and whom you serve and/or the products you offer?
- Can it be said more concisely?
- Does your mission statement explain clearly why the organization exists? Has it been updated? Does it need to be?

- Do you know how and when the existing mission statement came about? Was it changed from the original?
- Does it capture the essence of what you do?
- Does your mission statement relay your keen sense of purpose?
- Has it stood the test of time? Will it continue to?

Since your mission statement is vital to the organization's purpose and values, it's wise to review your mission statement regularly with the people who matter the most (e.g., staff, constituents, and boards).

For established mission statements, review your mission statement with a critical mindset. This should be done especially when you embark on strategic planning, merge with another business, rebrand, or want to reflect a new all-encompassing organizational strategy.

Examples of effective mission statements

The following mission statements are a marvel. None are over twenty words; most are easy to remember and clearly describe what the business provides.

- Public Broadcasting System (PBS): *To create content that educates, informs, and inspires.*
- Environmental Defense Fund: *To preserve the natural systems on which all life depends.*
- Patagonia: *Build the best product, cause no unnecessary harm, use business to inspire and implement solutions to the environmental crisis.*
- Smithsonian: *The increase and the diffusion of knowledge.*
- Watts of Love: *A global solar lighting nonprofit bringing people the power to raise themselves out of the darkness of poverty.*
- Ikea: *To create a better everyday life for the many people.*

- Khan Academy: *To provide a free world-class education for anyone, anywhere.*
- Jet Blue: *To inspire humanity—both in the air and on the ground.*
- Global Giving: *To transform aid and philanthropy to accelerate community-led change.*

The mission statements listed are from large organizations. They may have more of a capacity to create a concise and well-crafted mission. The organization that I founded created a two-paragraph mission statement. The process lasted well over four months. While I knew it was long (thirty-plus words) and relatively bulky, it was done in part with community assistance. Because of neighborhood involvement, I wasn't willing to find fault with this laboriously crafted mission.

Generate a mission statement that represents the heart of your organization yet is short and to the point. Include what you are doing to remedy the problems you are tackling. Produce a compelling statement that furthers your efforts to serve with excellence and moves the business forward.

For-profit business mission ideas to put into practice

- Mission statements with strong values can shape helpful organizational culture.
- The mission and its subsequent statement are rooted in the company's infrastructure.
- Inspirational mission statements can inspire others (e.g., employees, bosses, and more) to take positive action on behalf of the business.

Nonprofit business mission opportunities

- Understand the value of mission statement and the importance they have to the nonprofit field.
- A compelling mission statement describes your purpose, sets the tone for your business, helps identify your audience, and can move people to become supporters of your endeavor.
- The mission is key to the organization, so spend the time needed to develop a powerful, brief statement that captures the essence of your organization. Review it often.

More research on mission statements

- "What Is a Mission Statement?" Susan Ward, The Balance: Small Business, June 2020, https://www.thebalancesmb.com/mission-statement-2947996
- "Writing a Mission Statement for Your Team or Business," Indeed, https://www.indeed.com/hire/c/info/writing-a-mission-statement
- "What Is a Company Mission Statement and How Can You Create Your Own?" Lori Li, August 2020, https://www.tinypulse.com/blog/what-is-a-company-mission-statement-and-why-is-it-important
- "20 Effective Nonprofits Mission Statements," Sarah Henry, 2019, https://blog.elevationweb.org/20-effective-nonprofit-mission-statements
- "How to Develop a Mission Statement," https://www.thecompassforsbc.org/how-to-guides/how-develop-mission-statement
- "6 Tips for Writing a Perfect Nonprofit Mission Statement," April 2018, https://snowballfundraising.com/nonprofit-mission-statements/

Books

- *Your Simple Guide to Creating Mission, Vision and Value Statements*, Stuart Rice. LevelUpYourSales.com (2020).
- *101 Mission Statements from Top Companies: Plus Guidelines for Writing Your Own Mission Statements*, Jeffrey Abrahams. Ten Speed Press (2007).
- *Vision, Mission, Values, Aspiration, Do They Matter? A Business Professional's Guide to Drafting Vision/Mission Statements and Their Purpose*, Sam Schreim. Business Model Hackers (2020).

Chapter 12:
I CAN SEE CLEARLY NOW
Vision Statements

"Vision is seeing a future state with the mind's eye. Vision is applied imagination."

Stephen Covey, educator, author, and businessman

Vision Statement: *A vision statement is a sentence or short paragraph that succinctly describes the goals of a company, nonprofit, or some other entity. It states what you are trying to build and serves as a touchstone for your future actions.*

"What Is a Vision Statement," Susan Ward, on The Balance Small Business, thebalancesmb.com, June 23, 2020

The vision statement is vital because it reflects what the world would look like when your business meets all its goals. It is future oriented. Like a mission statement, it is ideally short, to the point, motivating, and/or inspirational. It uses a process for generating a vision statement you believe in. You need a mission *and* a vision statement because they have different purposes. A vision statement steers your thinking and doing in a positive direction.

A vision statement also speaks to your core competencies in addressing the organization's future. A mission statement tends to live in the present, while a vision statement is about what the future will look like if we do the right things now. Both a vision statement and a mission statement are relevant for most organizations.

Easy steps to understand a vision statement

Step 1: It is the vision or ideal future of the organization.

Step 2: The vision captures a clear, motivating statement.

Step 3: The vision statement reflects an exceptional future. It states what will happen when a business meets all of its goals.

Step 4: It should exist alongside your mission statement as an effective marketing tool.

A vision statement is an essential way to think about impact and why you are putting in this level of effort for a time yet to come. It also tells readers how the world would be different if you attained your objectives. Vision statements are forward-thinking in that they also speak to the impact your products, services, and goals and objectives have on your intended community.

A vision statement is a map of sorts. It assists you in getting to that ideal version of your organization. It also speaks to what you have to do to get there. The vision is the idea we see in our hearts and minds.

We know that aspirational statements are vital to have. The vision can harness the organization's services or merchandise power to make appropriate changes as we go along so the long-term goal is realized. A vision can speak to profits a company wants to make or the good nonprofits desire for our world.

A checklist for potential or current vision statements

- ✓ Does it offer a short, bold statement about what your organization hopes to accomplish in the long run?
- ✓ Is it transformational and future-oriented?
- ✓ Is it inspirational and/or motivational?
- ✓ Can you set standards of excellence with your vision statement?
- ✓ Does it capture the uniqueness of the business?
- ✓ Does it clarify the business's values, purpose, and direction?
- ✓ Can it speak to what the organization might achieve in ten, fifteen, or even twenty years?
- ✓ Have you used simple, concrete language and avoided jargon?
- ✓ Does your vision motivate others to take action, e.g., buy the product, join the team, expand your influence, and so on?
- ✓ What would our world look like if the challenge you are tackling with your business was solved?

Keep in mind the questions just mentioned because they can guide you in generating an effective vision statement. (You can use this exercise to create the mission statement as well. Simply substitute the word "mission" for "vision" in the appropriate places.)

Start creating or revising your vision statement using the exercise below:

- Write down two or three paragraphs about a possible vision, using suggestions from the questions listed. This exercise can be done alone or with a group.
- Highlight keywords.
- Summarize what you've written in a sentence or two.
- Take your time! Optimally, take however long you need, but set a target deadline.
- Let confidence shine through in the statement.
- Sit with it for a while.
- If you start doing it by yourself, do not restrict others' participation.
- Ask those critical to the business to vet it.
- Listen to their suggestions. Change it as needed.
- Make sure it resonates with others and captures what you do in a short, concise sentence.

Examples of creative vision statements that work

- The Humane Society: *A humane society.*
- The Brooklyn Academy of Music: *To be home to the adventurous artists, audiences and ideas.*
- Avon: *To be the company that best understands and satisfies the product, service and self-fulfillment needs of women globally.*
- Feed the Children: *Create a world where no child goes to bed hungry.*

- Human Rights Campaign: *Equality for everyone.*
- Oxfam: *A just world without poverty.*
- Make-A-Wish Foundation: *That people everywhere will share the power of a wish.*
- Sony: *To be a company that inspires and fulfills your curiosity.*
- Oceana: *Seeks to make our oceans as rich, healthy and abundant as they once were.*
- Nike: *Bring inspiration and innovation to every athlete in the world.*

More on vision statements

No matter how long you have been at an organization, or what role you play, know your mission and vision statements and company values. They are a representation of the work provided to your community. It is the reason you are in business. A vision is as fundamental to an enterprise as water is to (most) plants.

The shortfalls mentioned most often in the literature regarding the creation of vision statements are that they can be too similar and not specific enough.

I recommend creating both the mission and vision statement in a relatively close timeframe as it will help ensure they are unique yet related. While the two statements have different purposes and are not interchangeable, they are of equal importance. Both vision and mission statements inspire and move customers, employees, potential participants, and board members to act on your behalf.

Test your knowledge

Answer these true and false questions about mission and vision statements.

1. It is possible that your mission and vision statements can be interchangeable.

   Answer: False: Your mission statement is in the "here and now" and addresses what your organization does and why it exists. Your vision statement is future oriented. It says this is what the world would look like if all of your goals were met.

2. It's crucial to change your mission statement after ten years or longer.

   Answer: False: A mission statement is your ongoing identity, so change it only if and when it seems appropriate. It is valuable to review your mission statement regularly. For example, it may no longer reflect the community you serve. Or maybe you have merged with another organization, your products have been altered significantly, or your mission statement was never right in the first place.

3. The community you serve does not have to be involved in the crafting of your mission and/or vision statement. It just adds another level of work for the organization's staff.

   Answer: False: If you adhere to a participant-driven service model, you must have community members involved on some level in defining the organization's mission and vision. The people you are offering services should offer their stamp of approval on something as vital as a mission and/or vision statement. This is empowerment in action.

4. Word count for a mission and vision statement doesn't matter as much as the actual content and how well they summarize your organization.

Answer: False: Word count does matter. A lengthy mission or vision statement is the antithesis of what it should be. Twenty words is about right. Think of it as a kind of tagline that gives you a sense of the organization right away. A mission or vision statement over thirty to thirty-five words is too long for its purpose.

For-profit vision ideas to put into practice

- Values and implementing them are more important than ever. It is mandatory that anyone in a profit-making company understands the importance and acts upon these concepts moving forward.
- Mission and vision statements are integral in business. They can function as a compass and inform the business of an appropriate direction.
- Although many for-profit businesses are realizing the significance of having a mission statement, a vision statement hasn't been as essential. The for-profit sector has been waking up to the value of having a vision statement.

Nonprofit vision opportunities

- To get the biggest bang from your buck, make sure your values are represented by your vision statement.
- Let your vision statement help with decisions concerning the future of the organization.
- Having a vision statement keeps in mind the agency's priorities and can motivate it toward an expectational future

More research on vision statements

- "What Is a Vision Statement?" Sean Peek, Business News Daily, December 2019, https://www.businessnewsdaily.com/4533-business-plan-outline.html
- "How to Write a Vision Statement: Your Go-To Guide," Amanda Atrash, Clear Point Strategy, https://www.clearpointstrategy.com/how-to-write-a-vision-statement-why-that-isnt-enough/
- "How to Write a Good Vision Statement for 2022, Step-by-Step + Examples," Tom Wright, Cascade.app, https://www.cascade.app/blog/write-good-vision-statement
- "How to Write a Nonprofit Vision Statement that Will Shape Your Organization's Future," Alyssa Conrardy, Prosper Strategies, January 31, 2021, https://prosper-strategies.com/write-nonprofit-vision-statement-will-truly-shape-future/
- "How to Craft a Vision Statement That Will Guide Your Nonprofit," BoardBuild Team, August 27, 2020, https://www.boardbuild.org/how-to-craft-a-vision-statement-that-will-guide-your-nonprofit/

Books

- *The Visual Vision Statement Workbook-Business Edition: Your Guide to Create Your Corporate Vision Statement*, Adriana Girdler. CornerStone Dynamics (2020).
- *Developing the Non-Profit Infrastructure: A Step-by-Step Guide on How to Write an Effective Mission Statement, Vision Statement, Organization History and Program Description*, Amber Wynn. CRG Enterprises (2015).
- *The Wilder Nonprofit Field Guide to Crafting Effective Mission and Vision Statements*, Emil Angelica. Fieldstone Alliance (2013).

- *Build a Better Vision Statement: Extending Research with Practical Advice*, Shelley A. Kirkpatrick. Lexington Books (2016).
- *Vivid Vision: A Remarkable Tool for Aligning Your Business Around a Shared Vision of the Future*, Cameron Herold. Lioncrest Publishing (2020).

Chapter 13:
INTENTIONAL THINKING
Strategic Thinking

"Strategic planning is not strategic thinking. Indeed, strategic planning often spoils strategic thinking causing managers to confuse real vision with the manipulation of numbers."

Henry Mitzenberg, Canadian academic and author on business and management

Strategy: *A business strategy is an outline of the actions and decisions a company plans to take to reach its business goals and objectives.*

Indeed.com

Strategic Thinking: *Strategic thinking focuses on finding and developing unique opportunities to create value by enabling a provocative and creative dialogue among people who can affect a company's direction.*

"What Is Strategic Thinking?" effectivegovernance.com.au

> ***Strategic Planning:*** *The art of creating specific business strategies, implementing them, and evaluating the results of executing the plan, in regard to a company's overall long-term goals or desires.*
>
> The Center for Applied Research, interpersonalskillsonline.com

What is this material concerning strategy, strategic thinking, and strategic planning all about? These three sound similar and seem complicated. You may be asking, "Are you sure I really need it?" The short answer is yes, you do.

In business it is essential to plan your future, since you depend on it. These strategic models (e.g., strategy, strategic thinking, and strategic planning) are included in this chapter.

I advocate strongly for strategic thinking as opposed to strategic planning. It is adaptable, occurs in the now, is ongoing, and written in understandable language. You need to have strategic thinking to attempt strategic planning. So why not incorporate it as a regular practice at your company?

For ages, if you wanted to perform long-range planning, there was one tried-and-true method with which to do so—called strategic planning. In this chapter, I plunge into strategic planning first and then speak to why its relevancy is not necessarily the tool for today. Then I explore strategic planning alternatives that might prove helpful.

- funding
- strategic question(s)
- strategic planning group
- facilitator
- strategic planning document
- strategic planning process
- writing a potential grant to fund the strategic plan
- measurable goals

Strategic plans

A strategic plan identifies tactics that will enable the business to advance its mission and/or values through measurable goals in a defined period. It provides direction through these actionable, measurable goals. The planning looks at external and internal factors.

It commonly uses a SWOT analysis, which identifies an organization's Strengths, Weaknesses, Opportunities, and Threats. Typically, the strategic planning process is led by a consultant versed in strategic planning. There are meetings or retreats in collaboration with the board, staff, and sometimes with invested collaborators. The conventional wisdom suggests that the plan be suitable for three to five years.

Strategic planning was initially derived during World War II and described the methodology used to create tactics to win a war. Not long afterward, corporations adopted strategic planning to create a blueprint for success.

It gave way to a whole new industry of consultants, methodologies, and computer programs on how to plan strategically. My research found that nonprofits chose strategic planning in the mid-1980s. It is now widely accepted and, in some cases, a required practice.

Let's first look at the positives of strategic planning and why you might consider using this method of forecasting.

Reasons for undertaking a strategic plan

- You just had a significant change in leadership, and you want to help the organization know where it's headed.
- You have recently expanded, added a significant product, merged, or radically changed directions.
- A strategic plan has helped your business in the past and you want to use it for creating more profits.
- You believe wholeheartedly in the strategic planning process and think it's useful for the business to implement one every three to five years.
- Nonprofit funders are asking the organization to implement a strategic plan and will give you the money to do so.
- It is considered by many in the business world to be a best practice.
- It can hopefully motivate staff and board to grasp the organization's vision, mission, and values, while fostering communication and inclusiveness.
- You know of a great process and an even better consultant/facilitator.

Is strategic planning problematic?

Now let's turn to the challenges of strategic planning and speak to why it might not be the cure it was billed to be. In 1994, Henry Mintzberg wrote an influential article in the *Harvard Business Review* entitled, "The Fall and Rise of Strategic Planning." He argued that strategic planning often discourages strategy. "Sometimes, strategies must be left as broad visions, not precisely articulated, to adapt to a changing environment."

He further stated that: "[W]e must liberate strategy from the confines of a constrained and defined planning process and foster a culture that encourages strategic thinking at every level of an organization. Strategy needs to be unbound from pedestrian and conventional thinking." (See end of chapter for resources.)

I recall from personal experience that some folks involved in the strategic planning process really liked it. It can develop camaraderie and makes people feel productive and accomplished. In some foundations that support nonprofits financially, it has been recommended as a best practice. It also yields impressive outcomes on paper.

Yet, it has numerous drawbacks. These plans are supposed to be like the ox (strategic plan) that is harnessed to the cart (business) and pulls you toward your optimum future. It appeared that strategic planning might be able to do a lot of heavy lifting.

Why, if it's so vital, does a lengthy strategic plan sit on someone's office shelf gathering dust? This is after it's laboriously tackled and set in place at considerable time and costs. The answer to the question is complicated since it's customary to plan for an organization's future.

Strategic planning can be problematic. For starters, it's not the most agile of methods, and it takes a considerable amount of time and money. It demands that various resources be in place, including staff, board members, department heads, and possibly community partners.

Also, it needs a facilitator and a planning process that will lead you to strategic issues and solutions. The trickiest part of strategic planning may be *that it doesn't seem to deliver the all-important strategic direction and has very limited accountability*. Outcomes and goals, yes; however, it's not exactly what the process is in place for. It can also take months to write the plan up, so by the time it is ready, people have forgotten what they said they were going to do.

In this chapter the focus is less on strategic planning and instead includes and tracks regular strategic thinking and strategic agendas. Business plans, which many organizations already do, are also an acceptable practice (covered in this book).

First strategic plan

As you may remember from an earlier chapter, I called multiple funders and finally got one who said: "I will give you $5,000 to create a strategic plan, and if that works out well, we may give you more money." Even though I wasn't sure this was what I wanted, I decided to run with this opportunity.

As mentioned, there are legitimate complaints regarding strategic planning; however, the promise for more funds plus building community were all the reasons I needed to get started.

I realized that in order to meet the goal of empowerment, the community would have to help mold the center's goals and outcomes. People's opinions mattered. It was vital to give individuals avenues to create a healthy community for raising children.

This was an advantageous version of strategic planning because of the community input. It is called a "bottom-up" plan, meaning that the invested participants at the time were involved in an essential portion of the process. They spoke to us about what they wanted to see in the next three to five years. In addition to strategic planning, we, as a group, crafted the mission and vision statement for our center.

Several years went by after we submitted our plan to the foundation that funded us. We hadn't heard from them. Then, seemingly out of the blue, I got a phone call from the foundation. There was a new program officer named Corinne. She said she was reviewing grantee files and came across our strategic plan.

Corinne said it was rare to see so much community involvement in a plan and to see it as successfully executed as ours. She seemed genuinely impressed. Corinne set a time to meet us and felt hopeful she could get us a grant for program operations.

I was happy that she appreciated all the hard work that went into creating these strategies. I also liked that she was supportive of this plan that involved people in the neighborhood. She concluded with saying we deserved additional financial support from the foundation.

That was the beginning of a prosperous, long-term funded partnership. Corrine not only gave us a beneficial operating grant, but the foundation supported the center with substantial donations for ten plus years.

While strategic planning can work in some circumstances, it is generally burdened with shortcomings.

Problems with strategic planning

- Not fluid or flexible enough in today's fast-paced environment.
- Can be expensive.
- Most often will have to hire a facilitator.
- Is limited by a time frame.
- Can be a very lengthy and onerous process.
- Impressive outcomes on paper that don't translate well to the issues facing a business.
- Does not necessarily deliver the promised strategic directives.

- Language of the strategic plan can be full of jargon and not easy to understand.
- Often lacks practical applications.
- After completion, it may sit untouched in someone's office closet for a long time.
- Very limited accountability for the organization to implement the strategic plan.

Five myths about strategic planning

Now, let's test your knowledge to find out some of the misconceptions regarding strategic planning. What follows are common myths about strategic planning. Each of these statements contains something inherently false. While this might be obvious, it is problematic that some feel strategic planning offers a cure for organizational struggles.

1. Strategic planning does not necessarily incorporate your mission and vision.
   Answer: Strategic planning incorporates your mission and vision. It is crucial to the process. By doing so, it clarifies your organizational sense of purpose.

2. Your strategic plan will start producing results soon after completion.
   Answer: Unfortunately, your strategic plan will not automatically produce results. You have to implement the strategies that came out of the planning project. It often takes quite a bit of time before you see results, if any.

3. A strategic plan can be valid for up to five years.
   Answer: A strategic plan usually does not last three, let alone five years these days. It can be amended if most of your outcomes have not been met, and these outcomes are still relevant. The new standard for strategic planning has become

two years. The goal is to have a shorter plan because it helps an organization become fluid and flexible and able to change strategies (if necessary).

4. The best and most effective strategic plans come from a practiced strategic planner/facilitator.
   Answer: It helps to have an experienced strategic facilitator, but there is only so much one person can do. The burden is on the organization to apply the strategies that you come up with during the planning process. The facilitator will not be responsible once the plan is written and you sign the final check for their work. A seasoned facilitator should offer clear directives on how to implement the plan and suggest in what manner you need to revisit it.
5. Strategic planning and strategic thinking are basically the same.
   Answer: Strategy is strategy, but strategic thinking is not strategic planning and vice versa. They are different, but strategic planning couldn't exist without strategic thinking.

Strategic thinking: A unique approach to strategizing

What does "strategic thinking" mean to you? Take a moment to process this question before you move forward. "Strategic thinking is the ability to accurately assess your environment, forecast changes, and use the data to orchestrate opportunities to amplify your impact," according to Elsa Rios, principal of Strategies for Social Change, LLC (strategiesforsocialchange.com), in *Building a Strategic Thinking Organization, A Toolkit.* How does this happen?

The comprehensive toolkit suggests three significant methodologies:

- Environmental Awareness and Strategic Foresight

- Out-of-the-Box Thinking
- Agility and Adaptability

(See end of chapter for resources.)

I agree with these three points. To paraphrase, environmental knowledge, critical thinking skills, and flexibility alongside resilient action is strategic thinking at its best. These tools are helpful for planning for future challenges and unexpected predicaments.

When we consider strategic thinking, one size doesn't fit all. And what works today might not work tomorrow. Adaptability is key. This is a sure way for business to construct a beneficial future.

Strategic thinking encompasses a holistic, tactical way to see the work, its challenges, and what lies ahead. Acting strategically is innovating the way we plan. It helps streamline our processes and leverage opportunities and issues as they come up.

Thinking strategically indicates the need for planning to be ongoing, not just carried out during strategic planning every three to five years.

Trends and policy changes in funding and an insecure purchasing environment all mean that a business must be in the position of regularly adjusting its views and beliefs. Strategic thinking can prepare us for what's to come with suppleness, determination, and inventiveness.

Imagine that strategic thinking is the process of active, daily visioning and problem solving. It is the practice of understanding life's tests, and how you will use them to move the business toward its goals. One of the ways to get there is to start asking questions.

Questions to kick-start strategic thinking

- Is the organization heading in the right direction? How do you know this?
- If you were to freeze this moment in time, where will the business be in two years (if you keep going in this direction)?
- Can your organization course-correct swiftly if need be?
- Do you feel you and your staff read the trends well and anticipate new developments?
- How much is your organization adhering to your original mission and vision statement?
- Can your organization respond quickly to opportunities?
- Are you on track to meet nonprofit funder goals? Sales goals? Organizational goals?
- Do you adjust your beliefs and attitudes as the intents change?

Please add your own questions/concerns to the list as needed.

Generating the appropriate queries for your organization can help form strategies. Applied and focused tactics can enable you to steer your course. It is imperative that we understand, through a variety of strategic thinking methodologies, where we would like the organization to be in the future. Deliberate, conscious thinking is a way to reason and act differently than what we are all used to.

This additional quote from Elsa Rios sums up strategic thinking perfectly:

"It will take courageous leadership to construct more strategic organizational models. The task will require relinquishing the old mental models that we often hold as 'absolute truths,' tolerating the discomfort of 'not knowing' and a fierce commitment to building inquisitive leaders throughout the organization."

(See end of chapter for resources.)

I am not offering a color-by-numbers set of instructions for strategic thinking; however, I think a sampling of approaches might be helpful. These methods work to reinforce strategic thinking.

Consider a careful analysis of strategic options. Speak with others who may be interested in strategic thinking or have tried it out. It's time to get in front of the curve to see how your organization might benefit from using a form of regular strategic thinking.

Compare and contrast strategic thinking and strategic planning

Now that you have an idea how strategic planning and strategic thinking function, we will compare strategic thinking to strategic planning. Pick what would work best for your organization. Understand there are many benefits that effective planning can achieve for your organization.

Strategic thinking

1. It occurs in the now. A specific time frame doesn't limit it.
2. It speaks in understandable terms about problems and issues that are currently occurring and that may continue in the future.
3. It is not time limited. You can devise and update strategies as you go.
4. It is cost-effective.
5. Facilitation can be done in-house.
6. The blueprint you create is very fluid and flexible.
7. It is ongoing.
8. It involves whoever would be valuable to the planning process (e.g., staff, department heads, board members).
9. It is nontraditional. It is based on out-of-the-box thinking.
10. It adapts well to changing circumstances.
11. It consists of written plans, outlines, and agendas to present weekly, biweekly, and so on as trackers and reminders.
12. A series of ongoing questions (that can change) helps frame your process of strategic thinking.

Strategic planning

1. It looks three to five years in the future.
2. It typically uses industry jargon and sophisticated language. It may not deal with current issues unless they are part of the strategic plan. The strategic plan usually comes with a set of goals that need to be implemented.
3. It is time-limited.
4. It can be expensive.
5. A facilitator is hired (in most cases).
6. You need to stick with the plan and the strategic objectives.
7. There are meetings, conferences, or all-day retreats that solidify your work.
8. It is formalized and can involve staff (usually a CEO), board members, and others (as applicable).
9. It is traditional.
10. The information culled by the strategic planning process is not necessarily adaptable, or accountable, and has a fixed structure it adheres to.
11. Written plans are received months down the line to remind people of what they are going to do and how the organization is going to change.
12. A few well-crafted questions help frame your strategic planning effort.

Options for strategic thinking

Apply strategies that don't impose unnecessary hardships on a business. The primary concept that works toward this goal is strategic thinking in all its expressions. It uses generative (productive) thinking, which is reviewing and problem-solving the issue that the organization is trying to remedy.

Strategies that I've included as alternatives are adaptive strategy, matrix mapping, and strategic agendas. There is a whole field of options that exists other than strategic planning that you can find on the internet. We already know how important it is to look ahead and plan. Think about applying one of these strategies or something else you come across related to strategic thinking to enhance your organization's resourcefulness and long-term sustainability.

Adaptive strategy

Adaptive strategy is helpful in engaging your business circle in dealing with the issues it faces. This is an invitation to add more voices to the mix. It's time to get outside of your own frame of reference and get fresh new ideas. Adaptive strategy shows that with support from the employees in the organization, you can come up with fitting resolutions to challenges and plan for the future.

In 2013, the *Stanford Social Innovation Review* published a thought-provoking article on strategic planning by Dana O'Donovan and Noah Rimland Flower, entitled "The Strategic Plan Is Dead. Long Live Strategy." The subtitle is "In Today's Fast-Changing World, Why Freeze Your Strategic Thinking in a Five-Year Plan?" This is an informative article about reinventing strategy for our planet today. The authors wrote:

"The world has become a more turbulent place, where anyone with a new idea can put it into action. This has left organizational leaders with a real problem since the trusted, traditional approach to strategic planning is based on assumptions that no longer hold. The static strategic plan is dead. We think that what is necessary today is a strategy that breaks free of static plans to be adaptive and directive, that emphasizes leaning and control and that reclaims the value of strategic thinking for the world that now surrounds us."

(See end of chapter for resources.)

The authors suggested a concept they call adaptive strategy. "Instead of the old approach of making a plan and sticking to it, which led to centralized strategic planning around fixed time horizons," the authors believe in:

- Setting a direction and testing it.
- Treating the whole business as a team that is experimenting with its way to success.

This methodology holds much promise, as many in the business sector see clear limitations on the traditional strategic plan.

"Conversational Leadership goes into detail about open adaptive strategy. Unless the conversations are open to others traditionally not included, the strategy won't be accommodating or flexible enough."

conversational-leadership.net
(See end of chapter for resources.)

The Stanford article speaks to this by advising, "Treat the whole organization as a team."

This open adaptive strategy resonates since the goal for the entire organization is empowered employees who in turn can value others. It promotes learning and openness to other viewpoints besides that of senior staff and the board.

Open adaptive strategies support:

"Improved communication, enhanced decision making, increased commitment and engagement from more people."

conversational-leadership.net.
(See end of chapter for resources.)

Think about adaptive strategy

- Are people in your organization open to new approaches other than strategic planning, like adaptive strategy?
- Would you consider doing further research on adaptive strategy to see if it can work for your business?
- What are the strengths and weaknesses of adaptive strategy as applied to your organization?
- Do you see where strategic thinking is part of adaptive strategy? Why or why not?
- Why would additional voices create more effectiveness (in adaptive strategy)?
- What does conversational leadership mean to you?

Matrix mapping

Matrix mapping is a cost analysis process integrated with understanding the value of an organization's program, product, and/or service. A noteworthy book that inspired this approach is called *Making Strategic Decisions for Financial Viability* by Jeanne Bell, Jan Masoka, and Steve Zimmerman. (See end of chapter for resources.)

It lays out a matrix map that determines financial impact on each program/service/product you offer. In addition, part of the planning is to aid staff, community, or board in understanding the impact a particular program or product has on the people you serve.

It asks relevant questions like: Do people like this service and use it? Is it a vital program or product for everyone concerned? Is it cost effective? Does the staff think it works? It assesses the mission impact of each program you run. It can simultaneously be a business and a financial tool. You see the results as you chart them on the matrix map.

It was used as one methodology (out of two) in the 2013 strategic plan I was involved in. It gave us a unique perspective on programs and services. And doing it was fun. It creates a straightforward look at what an organization contributes to a particular group of people through their products or services.

Be prepared to use the company's resources (primarily fiscal and time) to have it benefit the organization. Before you convene a meeting of staff, board, and/or community reps, conduct a cost analysis of every product, program, or service you run. After this process is complete, assemble a staff meeting (or whomever you deem helpful) to determine where each program fits on the matrix map.

The outcome of the matrix map ought to be shared with notable parties (e.g., directors, participants, service partners, and consumers). It gives business a bird's-eye view of what's working and what isn't. It is a useful process to understand each service or product through a fiscal and mission-driven process that provides insight and subsequent directive action.

This was created for nonprofits to give them an idea of what programs and services were working (or not) for the organization and the community they serve. It seems versatile enough that it could be applied to either departments within corporations or small business. It is an engaging and thoughtful process.

Think about matrix mapping

- Is it clear how matrix mapping applies strategic thinking?
- Is this a process that will benefit your business? Why or why not?
- Are your programs mission driven or motivated by something else? How can you more closely align these services with your values?
- What do you think the advantages are if you apply matrix mapping to your nonprofit?
- How do you think knowing about program financial viability might help your nonprofit?

(Strategic) learning agendas

The learning agenda is a tactical questioning process that examines core issues facing an organization. Asking appropriate questions can generate vital actions that lead to outcomes. Brainstorming can help start the process of getting at the vital questions. The results of this querying process can facilitate learning and beneficial decision-making.

This method of asking questions and learning should be ongoing. If this sounds familiar, it should be, as it is what strategic thinking is set up to do. It can be more fluid than strategic planning because it doesn't have to be as demanding, expensive, or time consuming.

Learning agendas ask you to formulate great questions to get at directional, strategic information that can move the company forward. Therefore, I am recommending a version of strategic thinking (which this is). These agendas are a helpful way to address topic-specific areas or even multiple concerns. How broad you make the subject is up to you.

A learning agenda involves senior staff, department heads, participants, and more. Just as participant-driven services are a way to empower people, so, too, are strategic learning agendas. It can replace a regularly held meeting if there are issues that need to be solved.

Stakeholders can help to identify significant areas and give evidence that improves results and operations. In this way, the learning agenda can foster a culture of knowledge and ongoing advancement. It identifies where gaps in understanding are and what still needs to be comprehended.

Think about strategic learning agendas

- Would you use a strategic learning agenda at your organization? Why or why not?
- What did you like/not like about it?
- In what ways might you modify it so it would work for your organization?
- How might you position a strategic learning agenda so that people understand it or want to use it?
- Why is it essential to use the questioning process in strategic thinking?

Strong reasons to implement a learning agenda

Develop strategic thinking for troubleshooting, problem solving, or absorbing information that supports ongoing learning. As the US AID Learning Lab notes, you can use it to bridge knowledge gaps or inefficiencies. And most significantly, understand how sufficient knowing guides a team decision when action is needed (go to usaidlearninglab.org and search for "learning agenda"). (See end of chapter for resources.)

Learning agendas and other strategic thinking models tell us that we need to use the right kind of planning for the challenges that our organization faces. Learning agendas are appropriate for finding creative resolutions to organizational dilemmas.

How to use strategic thinking

- Clearly understand what strategic thinking is and its capacity for accomplishing what you need.
- Use strategic thinking tools to help track the process, problems, and potential solutions.
- Use strategic thinking regularly and for challenging issues the business is facing.
- Obtain solutions through asking clarifying, innovative questions that align with the mission and vision of the organization.
- The queries in the strategic thinking process ought to include the what, why, and how of the issue.
- Know where to focus premium company attention and how to let go of areas that aren't as crucial.
- Map out the problems so you can clearly see appropriate solutions.

- Brainstorm particular antidotes and prioritize these objectives. Modify as needed.
- Don't let concerns stop you from taking calculated risks, seeking advice, learning from others, observing trends, and asking suitable questions.
- Use innovation, empathy, agility, and knowledge in the strategic thinking process.

Another pass at strategic planning

For the twenty-five years that I was executive director of a nonprofit, the organization implemented four kinds of strategic designs. One was the initial, traditional strategic plan. The positives slightly outweighed the negatives because it was helpful for the relationship between the nonprofit and the community being served.

There were a number of benefits to strategic planning. They were as follows:

- The community was involved in every part of it.
- The participants helped create mission and vision statements.
- The process deepened our relationship with the neighbors.
- It gave us a heightened sense of direction.
- The strategic planning positioned us to receive more funding from the local foundation.

However, there were also drawbacks to strategic planning. They included the following:

- The strategic planning process took months to complete.
- It took even longer to implement.
- It was expensive (at the time).

- It was time consuming.
- It did not use everyday language.
- It was not agile or responsive to new issues or problems that surfaced.

Three out of the four strategic opportunities I participated in were nontraditional. One of them was field-testing for a strategic planning facilitator in 2007. It was a half-day training on applying strategy. The instruction was meant to be a learning process, yet I didn't retain much of it and used even less.

The second of these nontypical strategies was offered through our government funder. They spent an afternoon teaching us the standard business tool of SWOT (strengths, weakness, opportunities, and threats) analysis (referenced earlier in this chapter).

We had used SWOT in the initial strategic plan I was part of, so I and others at the organization knew and understood it. SWOT is an acceptable strategy to speak to the environmental issues affecting a business. However, the time dedicated to this meeting might have been spent more productively.

The last atypical strategic plan I helped produce was in 2013, a two-year plan that combined the approach in David La Piana's book *Business Strategies and Nonprofit Sustainability* and *Making Strategic Decisions for Financial Viability* by Bell, Masoka, and Zimmerman (referenced in Chapter 9).

This strategic plan was different than the established process because it combined several approaches. I felt that if I was going to undertake something like this, it would have to be relevant, pioneering, and what we needed to learn. I had too many contemporaries who spent a ton of money and time on the process, only to ignore their strategic plan after it was complete. These plans lacked overall usefulness and once it's finished, it doesn't have accountability for implementation.

Although I thought it was helpful to link strategies, we still spent $25,000 on the consultant, planning, and community meetings. It also took time to write up the ideas, including mapping out what we needed to do. This work plan was vital since it was ensuring that the next several years' strategic blueprint was implemented.

Several years after this strategic planning process was complete, we bought a second building for our branch office. A few staff members (including me) were overwhelmed by raising money for the renovation of the new building, which was upwards of several million dollars. The board at the time was anxious that we did not have a current strategic plan.

The capacity to tackle a whole new strategic plan was nonexistent. Luckily, the existing strategic plan still had useful directives in it, plus the ability to adapt and move us toward the future.

To achieve a modified plan, the staff and I looked at the strategic planning project as a whole and revised it. Our two overarching strategic questions and most of the work plan still applied to issues we wanted to give attention to. We used a type of adaptive strategy instead of tackling further strategic planning.

Implementing an adaptive approach helped us come up with strategies to deal with noteworthy issues without reinventing the wheel. For the organization I was working with, it was not the time to embark on a time-consuming, expensive, grant-seeking, less-than-supple strategic plan.

A vital takeaway is that there are excellent alternatives to strategic planning. These approaches mentioned are not nearly as time-consuming as the traditional process. However, it is important to keep a record of all your strategic thinking sessions.

Experts stress that the most critical outcome of strategic planning is to instill strategic thinking in the organization, which leads to strategic action by management. Strategic thinking encourages asking questions; using your creativity, imagination, and inspiration; having vision; and being fluid and adaptable. It gives direction without imposing hardships.

For-profit strategic thinking ideas to put into practice

- Exercise strategic thinking for setting direction of the future of the organization.
- Harness the tool of strategic thinking since it is supple, not nearly as time consuming (as strategic planning), builds good questioning skills, and can develop intentional long-range strategies.
- Advance strategic thinking to bridge knowledge gaps or inefficiencies.

Nonprofit strategic thinking opportunities

- Use strategic thinking techniques to cultivate the future of the organization.
- Give credibility to the up-and-coming strategic thinking approaches described or do your own research to find the right fit for your planning.
- Try implementing some form of strategic thinking, (maybe) an hour a week personally to see how it works. Afterwards, bring in a team, set ground rules, and tackle some of the issues you're confronting.

More research on strategic thinking

- "How to Cultivate Strategic Thinking Skills in 6 Steps," Pam Didner, August 8, 2020, https://pamdidner.com/develop-strategic-thinking-skills/
- "The Strategic Plan is Dead. Long Live Strategy," Dana O'Donovan and Noah Rimland Flower, *Stanford Social Innovation Review*, January 10, 2013, https://ssir.org/articles/entry/the_strategic_plan_is_dead._long_live_strategy
- "How Adaptive Strategy Is Adapting," Dana O'Donovan, Gabriel Kasper, and Nicole L Dubbs, *Stanford Social Innovation Review*, May 24, 2018, https://ssir.org/articles/entry/how_adaptive_strategy_is_adapting#
- "Building a Strategic Thinking Organization," Elsa Rios, Strategies for Social Change, https://www.strategiesforsocialchange.com/wp-content/uploads/2016/01/SSC-Toolkit2-FINAL-Email-11.20.15.pdf
- "Strategic Planning for Nonprofits," National Council of Nonprofits, https://www.councilofnonprofits.org/tools-resources/strategic-planning-nonprofits
- "Strategic Conversations," David Gurteen, in Conversational Leadership, https://conversational-leadership.net/strategic-conversations/
- Learning agendas, https://usaidlearninglab.org/

Books

- *HBR's 10 Must Reads on Strategy.* Harvard Business Review Press (2011).
- *Nonprofit Sustainability: Making Strategic Decisions for Financial Viability*, Jeanne Bell, Jan Masoka, and Steve Zimmerman. Jossey-Bass (2010).
- *How to Think Strategically, Sharpen Your Mind, Develop Your Competency, Contribute to Success*, Greg Githens. Maven House (2019).
- *Thinking Strategically: The Competitive Edge in Business, Politics and Everyday Life*, Avinash K. Dixit and Barry J. Nalebuft. W. W. Norton & Company (1993).
- *The Nonprofit Strategy Revolution: Real Time Strategic Planning in a Rapid-Response World*, 2nd Edition, David La Piana and Melissa Mendes Campos. Fieldstone Alliance (2018)
- *Strategic Planning: Understanding the Process (A BoardSource Toolkit).* BoardSource (2011).
- *Strategic Planning for Nonprofit Organizations: A Practical Guide for Dynamic Times*, Michael Allison and Jude Kaye. Wiley (2015).

Chapter 14: ACT "AS IF YOU'RE SUCCESSFUL"

Running a Successful Business

"Great organizations work with and through others to create more impact than they could ever do alone."

Forces for Good by Leslie Crutchfield and Heather McLeod Grant

Running Like a Successful Business: *Success is running a profitable enterprise that conducts business with honesty and integrity, makes meaningful contributions to the communities it serves and nurtures high-quality, balanced lives for its employees.*

Hope Wilson, senior marketing specialist at Skidmore, Owings and Merrill LLP as told to businessnewsdaily.com, Entrepreneurs Define the Meaning of Business Success

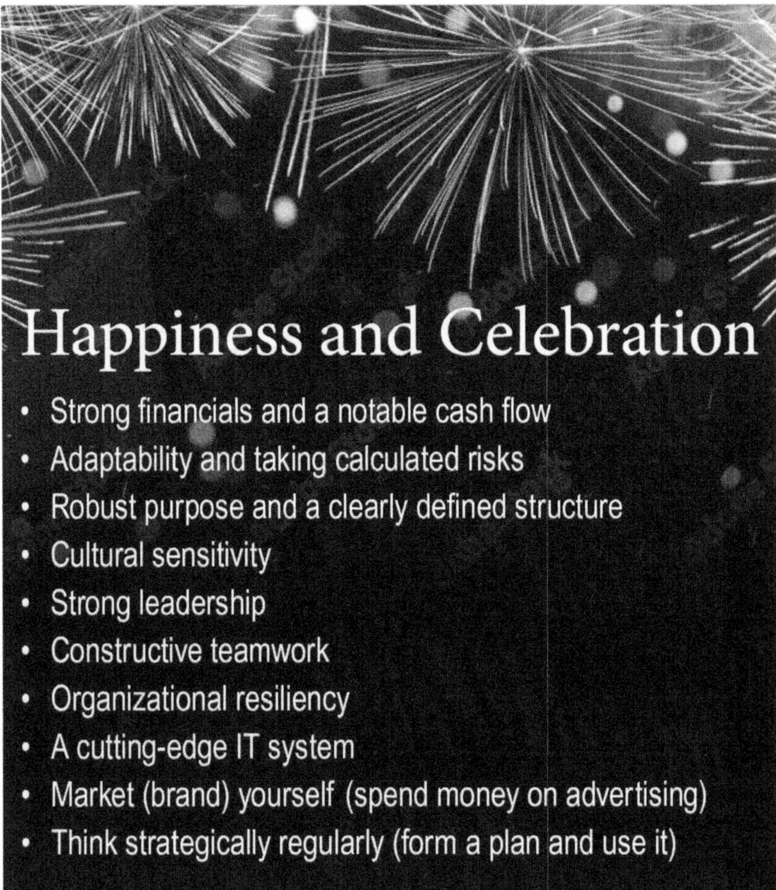

Running your organization as a successful business

Success is very subjective. It depends on how you define it. Some will say if the work you do allows happiness, then that's an accomplishment. Additionally, for achievement to occur in the future, for-profit businesses need to let their values be a guide.

Nonprofits have well-defined principles and could blend these with winning practices gathered from the for-profit sector. However, it is not going to work in future years for any business to continue blindly with a predictable method of doing business to reach the level of attainment that's possible.

For-profit business has historically been a leader when it comes to implementing practices that further profits. One could argue that these companies use solid measures to succeed. Nonprofits don't have a profit margin and are more interested in doing good work and implementing values.

Yet, numerous for-profit practices can be applied effectively (with adjustments) to nonprofits. Both business models can utilize each other's significant methodologies, possibly creating a hybrid approach to business.

You can Google what makes a business successful. Every "business authority" has a differing outlook on what makes a durable, thriving, long-lasting organization. Business executives often summarize their definitions in as few as three bullet points or as many as twelve.

Numerous aspects of effective business practice cross over from the for-profit to the nonprofit sectors. These include capacity building, sustainability, strategic planning, executive coaching, and how to run a successful business. To succeed in business today, you need quality planning (strategic thinking), strong operational and organizational skills, and flexibility. In Patrick Lencioni's book, *The Advantage: Why Organizational Health Trumps Everything Else in Business*, he says, "The ultimate competitive advantage is the health of the business." (See end of chapter for resources.)

How do we ensure a business is healthy and thriving?

It takes a collaborative effort, hardy staff, and the proper environment to have a successful enterprise. It is reassuring that experts in the for-profit world are promoting qualities such as effective and supportive teamwork, strong leadership, and adaptability.

Additionally, the list of high-performing business attributes includes an organization with a clearly defined purpose (e.g., strong mission or value and vision statements), beneficial communications, a tradition of feedback, cultural sensitivity, and loyalty.

What does running a successful business mean to you? List as many ways as you can to manage a thriving business (without giving up or sacrificing your mission, values statements, or charitable status).

It feels kind of flattering

Nonprofits are founded on ideological standards. When people find out I have worked for nonprofits for thirty-five years, they get excited and say, "I have always wanted to open a nonprofit. Do you want to hear about my fabulous idea for one?"

I am grinning because I appreciate people's enthusiasm and the desire to put their principles to good use. Yet, these folks often have a hazy view of what's involved in getting a charitable organization off the ground and running it as a business.

All people can think about is changing the world in accordance with their dreams. It can certainly start there. Yet, it is also important to realize that with any enterprise, you will have to face many formidable challenges.

It behooves us to treat a nonprofit like a business because it is. Best of all, you can build the organization's capacity to serve the community for generations to come. We truly need the inspiration and dedication to principles to move our world to a better place. But understand that any company needs to be run with the best professional standards that exist.

How to run a prosperous business

These are elements that determine an organization's health:

- Strong financials and an adequate cash flow.
- Adaptability and taking calculated risks.
- Robust purpose and a clearly defined structure.
- Cultural sensitivity.
- Strong leadership.
- Constructive teamwork.
- Organizational resiliency.
- A cutting-edge IT system.
- Marketing (branding) and spending money on advertising.
- Thinking strategically on a regular basis (form a plan and use it).
- Please add any other elements that are relevant to your organization.

At this point, it's important to pause and think about how to run a prosperous business. Brainstorm the elements you need or have seen that work to establish a successful business. I have compiled a list above, but what do you think is essential for business achievement?

Think about how to run a prosperous business

- Are there parallels between my list and yours regarding running a successful business? Which elements appeared on your list and mine?
- Are there aspects of your business that you need to strengthen?

- Are there areas on the list(s) that you have done well with to give yourself a pat on the back? What are those?
- Are there qualities on the list that you say your organization doesn't have? Why? Can you argue in favor of developing these qualities?

> *"According to 2019 data from the US Bureau of Labor Statistics, approximately 20% of new businesses fail during their first two years of being open, 45% during the first five years, and 65% during the first ten years. Only 25% of new businesses make it to fifteen years or more."*
>
> How to Run a Successful Small Business, Investopedia.com

We are talking about running a successful enterprise because even if we have a great idea for one, the labor statistics will tell you that 45 percent of businesses fail in the first five years. It is important to take note of the essential qualities that go into making a business sustainable and successful. We can learn from others.

Much like strategic thinking and sustainability, businesses need to have a mindset of continuous improvement and commitment to high performance. The next step is to put this information in a plan. Business experts say it should capture where you are going and how you are going to get there. Apply strategic thinking to generate your action steps (see Chapter 13).

Part of running your nonprofit establishment like a business is addressing the human aspects of growth and development at a company. A company needs to promote all facets of an employee's growth. The accent is on valuing employees and encouraging teamwork that builds trust, effective communications, and integrity.

Nonprofits can be reasonable in how they treat employees and implement values but are notorious for paying low wages. Yet, is that enough to have an effective business? The literature points out that it might not be. The trouble is that downgraded expectations about money are very real in many charitable circles. As William Clark has noted,

"Downgraded expectations affect the performance of nonprofits. Many nonprofits are influenced by the assumption that they are not a business and should not have strategic goals. Low expectations are supported by the idea nonprofits do not have a profit-generating model and should not worry about planning. There is a mindset that exists amongst them that scarce resources have to be divided among the many deserving organizations." (See end of chapter for resources.)

As you can see, Clark is alluding to the need for more strategic thinking around development (funding) and better processes for resource acquisition. Charities could gain a lot by changing their perspective from the scarcity mindset that there is never enough of the things we need, to the notion that there is enough of everything.

For-profits are challenged by their highly competitive nature and seem to exist in a dog-eat-dog world. They sometimes pretend they have values but they don't. Employees are unhappy and often a sense of value is lacking. The issues aren't as much about downgraded expectations but downgraded services and product quality.

Most of us have noticed that occasionally the product we love and have bought before falls apart soon after we purchase it. There can be a shortage of implemented values, a less-than-amiable company culture, not enough money, and inadequate marketing. How much the company is earning is often the crux of the matter for the stakeholder.

Both nonprofits and for-profits have formidable challenges to overcome. For-profits could learn that living by a set of values in the workplace offers compassion for the human condition and creates a better culture. Nonprofit staff could get more conscious of how they lower their expectations because they are in the charitable field that is always looking for money. These are major reasons to share effective strategies on how to succeed in the field of business.

Business plans

Business plans can tell us how to grow an organization from the beginning. They can explain why your particular business is necessary and how it will differ from competitors. A business plan (like other strategies mentioned in the book) can produce the beginnings of a winning enterprise.

The National Council of Nonprofits notes, "A business plan explains the who/what/how/where/when. It is used when a business is getting started or branching out and or looking for additional funding. It will typically answer questions like: 'Who are the customers? What is the geographic area for the services? What other companies are providing similar services? And what unique service does the business deliver?" (See end of chapter for resources.)

Both nonprofit and for-profit business plans contain very similar elements. While business plans can help a company to make profits, nonprofits can use business plans to expand their beneficial work. The helpful news is that you can choose the features of the plan that work best for your organization's purposes.

However, there are some unique differences in plans to meet requirements from each sector. Business plans can empower a company through the process of deciding on important aspects of the business.

Business planning is a way of answering questions about what goals the enterprise is trying to achieve or the questions it might answer. As you're building these plans, trust is an important quality to include, since it is a strong foundation on which to build. There are also basic strategic questions to help create a company plan that can lead you to the resources you need to succeed.

Checklist for an effective business plan

- ✓ An executive summary.
- ✓ Mission or company description. For-profits may not have a mission statement, but they might have a values statement and an organizational description.
- ✓ Market analysis.
- ✓ Competitive analysis.
- ✓ Products, services, and/or programs.
- ✓ Marketing and sales: For-profit businesses usually have this divided into two categories—marketing and sales—while nonprofits generally have a section on marketing but might call it outreach or networking.
- ✓ Operations or, in for-profit speak, how your organization is set up.
- ✓ Evaluation and assessment is the nonprofit description, while a for-profit measures its success by the funds brought in.
- ✓ Financial plan and projections.

(Checklist adapted from the Social Enterprise Business Plan by propelnonprofits.org and the Top 10 Components of a Good Business Plan by smartasset.com)

These are the vital components of a business plan that can help you to articulate a clear blueprint on how to move forward. It is important to note that while there are underlying similarities in these fundamentals of a business plan, each company differs in how it presents itself (e.g., what features go into the plan).

A cautionary tale of woe

It was the year 2000 at the nonprofit I ran. We were feeling good. We had recently purchased our 7,500-square-foot building with the help of the city government. I was raising money nonstop for the renovation of the additional 2,500 square feet we acquired when we bought the building, because it turned out the renovations would cost almost $500,000. I had already procured half of the capital, so it appeared from our financials that we were rolling in dough.

However, we were having trouble finding people who would work for a nonprofit. The Bay Area was in the middle of a dot-com boom originating in Silicon Valley. Young adults graduating from college were looking to cash in on this prosperous time, asking for starting salaries of $70,000. Back then, it was a little more than what I was making as a director of a nonprofit.

Our finance and operations guy, Rex, who had been with us part-time for a number of years, accepted a full-time job at an art nonprofit. He was straddling between the art organization and us. Not so well, I might add.

We posted a bookkeeper's job description with a competitive nonprofit wage. After four months, we started to worry when we weren't getting *any* candidates, even unqualified ones. So, Rex reached out to a friend who had a temporary employment firm. The standard placement fee came with a substantial reduction since he knew the owner.

We temporarily hired Kayla to work for us part-time. She seemed ready to roll up her sleeves and met the basic requirements of the bookkeeping job. Looking back and with hindsight being 20/20, Kayla was unqualified for the position. And most importantly, Rex didn't have the time to supervise her.

I was getting ready for a long, much-needed vacation. It was March 2002, and we had finally found someone we really liked to be our financial manager, Colleen. In the meantime, Kayla struggled with the job. We needed somebody who could work at a much higher level and who knew what s/he was doing with all our financial positions.

A few days before I was set to leave town, Rex came in to run a report for a funder that had given us money for the building renovation. He seemed undone when he came to my desk and asked why we were paying our architect almost $30,000 for the renovation. I swallowed hard and said, "I thought we capped her between $12,000 and $14,000."

"Here," he said, "I will show you the books." Of course, the proof was right there in the numbers. We had already paid our architect just under thirty thousand dollars. Rex asked our operations manager to pull the canceled checks that we paid her. In the meantime, I was going to meet with the architect the next day and ask her what happened.

I didn't have to wait until the following morning. That same afternoon, our operations manager laid out the checks. It seemed like there were dozens of them, which in and of itself was strange. I asked him how it was going, and he looked up with an odd expression and said, "Weird!" I asked what he meant. He motioned to a pile of checks and said, "These all have architectural stamps. This stack over here has none."

I turned over the checks that seemed suspicious and noticed that there was only one signature (there should have been two). It was meant to be my authorization, but instead was a bad forgery. I told Rex what I saw, and he advised me that I immediately run down to the bank a block away and ask what was going on. I did just that.

I spoke to the branch manager. After some long pauses, she said that the suspicious checks were being deposited in a personal account. This was followed by, "Do you know who Kayla is?" I cringed and replied, "She is our bookkeeper."

For us not to deal with Kayla's dishonest accounting a minute longer, I told her the very next morning over the phone that Rex was going to work with us the next few weeks until he trained the new person. I thanked her for her service but informed her that her assistance was no longer needed.

While she seemed nervous, she didn't put up a fight. We started an investigation with the police the same day I let her go. Months later, Kayla ended up in jail for embezzlement. It was a disturbing outcome for her, and it upended our finance department.

Fortunately, we recovered most of the money she stole. We told Colleen, the prospective finance manager, our theft story, giving her a chance to back out. To this day, I remember what she said. "Oh, that's a terrible shame, but I am well versed in preventing embezzlement and can be of service to the organization." Colleen was hired and became an incredible asset to our company.

Colleen revamped our finance department with more checks, balances, and internal controls than were considered normal for a small organization. The strangest thing to me was that we had had an outside audit done a few months before this startling financial deception came to light.

Oddly enough, the accountants who came in to perform an external audit didn't find problems. When I told them what had happened, they said the focus of the audit wasn't to detect fraud but to see if the company's financial statements were reasonably stated. According to cfo.com, "Audits almost never find fraud; the data shows that external audits find fraud only 4 percent of the time."

I became a strong proponent for understanding the entire business nature of an organization. Running the company with internal controls, policies, manuals, and systems in place is imperative. All told, this experience with fraud was a tough wake-up call. Internal controls are also an indispensable addition to running the establishment as the business it is. The National Council of Nonprofits describes internal controls as "financial management practices. … The goal of internal controls is to create business practices that serve as 'checks and balances' on staff (and sometimes board members) and/or outside vendors."

Use financial checks and balances to keep your financial administration healthy and able to weather any setbacks you may encounter. Amanda Tyler of the National Council of Nonprofits has noted: “It is important to re-evaluate financial management practices to ensure a culture of efficiency and accountability that govern the management of a business’s resources.” (See end of chapter for resources.)

Internal fraud can happen to any business. My story is a warning that the lack of systematic checks and balances, weak internal controls, inadequate supervision, and the wrong (or dishonest) personnel can spell chaos for an organization. Robust financial management is a must for a business hoping to achieve longevity and accomplish its purpose for existing.

Running the enterprise as a business, with the necessary components in place, can expand the agency’s existing toolkit. It allows upgraded expectations, trust building, strong financial management, calculated risks, and a comprehensive business plan for funding or producing new ventures. We can learn and become all the wiser by using the best techniques from the fields of for-profits and nonprofits. These useful practices can keep the quality of our business noteworthy.

For-profit running like a successful business ideas

- Have a commitment to continuous improvement to obtain high performance at your business and turn a profit.
- Create a resourceful infrastructure (operations). Choose your own methods or select some from the building blocks on what a healthy organization looks like (listed in this chapter).
- Use a business plan for a new business, merging with another enterprise or when you are making a radical change.

Nonprofit running like a successful business opportunities

- Is your nonprofit guilty of downgraded expectations on funding and other issues concerning the business? Start changing that mindset today.
- Pay your staff a living wage. Do not succumb to the nonprofit mentality that there is just not enough money to do so.
- This chapter is about how to run an effective business. Use the checklist to ensure you are doing just that and highlight (and work on) the ones that need some elbow grease.

More research on operating your business effectively

- "What Is the Definition of Success in Business?" Svetlana, Modest Ads, http://modestads.com/definition
- "5 Behaviors That Define Healthy Organizations," Bernhard Heine, https://www.businesstown.com/shows/thinking-ceo-bernie-heine/5-key-behaviors-define-healthy-successful-organizations/
- Business Planning for Nonprofits," National Council of Nonprofits, https://www.councilofnonprofits.org/tools-resources/business-planning-nonprofits
- "How to Run a Successful Small Business," Investopedia, https://www.investopedia.com/articles/pf/08/make-money-in-business.asp
- Audits, *CFO* magazine, https://www.cfo.com/?s=audits

- "Social Enterprise Business Plan," Propel Nonprofits, https://www.propelnonprofits.org/resources/social-enterprise-business-plan/
- "Introducing Strategic Thinking into a Nonprofit Organization to Develop Alternative Income Streams," William Clark, *Journal of Practical Consulting*, Fall/Winter 2012, https://www.regent.edu/acad/global/publications/jpc/vol4iss1/JPC_Vol4Iss1_Clark.pdf
- "Transforming Nonprofit Business Models," Propel Nonprofits, https://www.propelnonprofits.org/resources/transforming-nonprofit-business-models/
- "10 Tips for Running a Successful Nonprofit Organization," Jennifer Laszlow Mizrahi, *Huffington Post*, https://www.huffpost.com/entry/10-tips-for-running-a-suc_b_1631775
- "Why You Should Run Your Nonprofit Like a Business," The Modern Nonprofit, September 1, 2020, https://themodernnonprofit.com/run-nonprofit-like-business/
- "The Future of Nonprofits: Run Them Like an Innovative Business," Soren Kaplan, Inc., https://www.inc.com/soren-kaplan/the-future-of-non-profits-run-it-like-an-innovative-business.html

Books

- *The Advantage: Why Organizational Health Trumps Everything Else in Business*, Patrick Lencioni. Instaread
- *The Nonprofit Business Plan: A Leader's Guide to Creating a Successful Business Model*, Brent Copen, Lester Olmstead-Rose, David La Piana, and Heather Gowdy. Fieldstone Alliance (2012).

- *Managing the Nonprofit Organization: Principles and Practices,* Peter F. Drucker. Harper Business (2006).
- *How to Write a Business Plan,* Mike P. McKeever. NOLO (2018).
- *The Lean Start-Up*, Eric Ries. Jossey-Bass (2012).
- *Forces for Good: The Six Practices or High Impact Nonprofits,* Leslie Crutchfield and Heather McLeod Grant. Gildan Media, LLC (2008).

Chapter 15:
HAVE THE RIGHT INGREDIENTS FOR GROWTH
Capacity Building

"We want a world that works for everyone with no one, and nothing left out."

Buckminster Fuller

Capacity Building: *Whatever is needed to bring a business to the next level of operational, programmatic, financial, or organizational maturity, so it may more effectively and efficiently advance its mission into the future. Capacity building is not a one-time effort to improve short-term effectiveness, but a continuous improvement strategy toward the creation of a sustainable and effective organization.*

councilofnonprofits.org

Capacity building is the set of actions we take to make the organization effective, by adding to or improving the business functions. The interrelated areas that can produce accomplishments are infrastructure, operations, financial health, and services or products. Also, leadership advancement is included in numerous capacity lists. It is another approach to take for ensuring the business is healthy. It pays tribute to strong sustainability approaches.

It appears that in a for-profit, capacity building is often viewed as developing a leader's or a key employee's capabilities. These growth opportunities reside in Human Resources. It's thought of as the administrative side of business, since it's crucial to the budgeting process.

Capacity has been criticized in the private sector since it can be vague or overused. But regardless, it is critical to look at infrastructure with regularity since it can affect profits.

Capacity building is not the same for everyone. There is so much involved it's challenging to know where to begin. I recommend that you start at the place you know needs improvement, and move on from there.

It may be that your financial systems need adjusting. Doing so can positively impact your operations, so they function better. There is a connectivity between these major components, so it may not be as hard as you think.

Here is another helpful definition by the National Council of Nonprofits: "Capacity building refers to any intentional and sustained effort to improve an organization's functioning. When capacity building is successful, it strengthens the business's ability to fulfill its mission over time and to have a positive impact on lives and communities." (See end of chapter for resources.)

A maverick capacity-building opportunity

In 2005, I had the good fortune to apply for a capacity-building grant from local government. It was almost unheard of at the time, since growing an agency's capacity was not considered essential or cost-effective, especially with nonprofits. A woman named Beth managed the city-funding department at the time.

She was a rebel in all possible business ways. For starters, in the early 1990s, Beth originally thought up the funding that created a city grant department for nonprofits. She went to each of the city council members and told them about her idea for this funder department, which would be financed through a small annual property tax. The city council members considered her proposal to be a "pie in the sky" deal. And they were not the least bit interested in supporting Beth's passionate cause of creating a city funding department for children and their families. This didn't deter her.

She organized a significant number of children and parents to show up at City Hall on a designated date and time with full press coverage. Subsequently, the council members and many others sprinted to back her proposal and the property tax. Residents voted it in later that year. Clearly, Beth knew what she was doing.

After numerous years of running a dynamic children's advocacy organization, she negotiated with the mayor to assign her as the director of the funding department that she initiated. She succeeded.

After Beth had been in office for a year, she announced funding for an innovative proposal of capacity building for exemplary nonprofits. She was one of the first individuals I knew that provided a substantial, high-profile capacity-building grant.

The grant proposal was open to charitable organizations that could prove they helped their neighborhood by offering community programs that could demonstrate a need for expansion. I was excited to apply and strengthen the potential of the organization I founded.

The proposal asked nonprofits to assess local needs and decide on how to move forward with expanding the infrastructure. The project invited us to answer the question: "If the organization had an additional $xxx,xxx, how would you increase your capacity to grow your services?"

To do this, we hired a very competent writer, activist, and artist named Lauren. As per the grant directive, she conducted an extensive planning effort. Lauren interviewed hundreds of individuals (including youth) and held numerous focus groups with people who lived or worked in the neighborhood where the nonprofit was located. After months of preparation, and then writing the proposal, we pulled off an admirable application. We then had to defend it in front of a panel of judges.

We were thrilled to be one of five organizations that received these funds. The actual implementation of the grant was a lot of work, yet rewarding. Unfortunately, the "manna from heaven" (money) wasn't seen through the promised three years. Beth had moved on to start a consulting practice, so there was a new director of the funding office who nixed the last year of the funding.

It was a disappointing end to an amazing opportunity. However, I was pleased to discover the ins and outs of capacity building. I also had a chance to apply this knowledge firsthand. I hired a development manager because I finally had the money from the grant to do so. Building capacity to serve your community is vital. I cannot stress how important it is to understand operations through this elevated perspective.

Capacity building and staffing

Capacity building also relates to staffing and how we compensate and train people. Time and time again, nonprofits are really behind the curve on paying competent employees sustainable wages. It shows up a lot because top performers seek greener pastures when nonprofits simply cannot afford to pay higher wages (are downgraded expectations lurking again?). The lack of capacity can lead to deficiencies in key positions because of a money shortage.

In the business sector, people are mostly well compensated, but does poor compensation have to be the trade-off for working at a nonprofit? If you were to take a job with similar responsibilities in the nonprofit sector and compare the two, there would be huge disparities despite the hard work you put toward charitable employment. Salaries are a capacity issue. It's crucial to figure out where the middle ground lies with salaries between the profit and nonprofit fields.

Think about capacity building

- Does capacity building resonate with you? If so, how? If not, why not?
- Does capacity building seem cumbersome and just one more thing to do? Can you look at the components that comprise capacity building and determine which piece to tackle first?
- At your organization, what elements do you consider to be capacity building?
- Have you been working on capacity building without knowing it? What does that look like?
- Do you think capacity building is a strategic process? Why?

Overhead costs

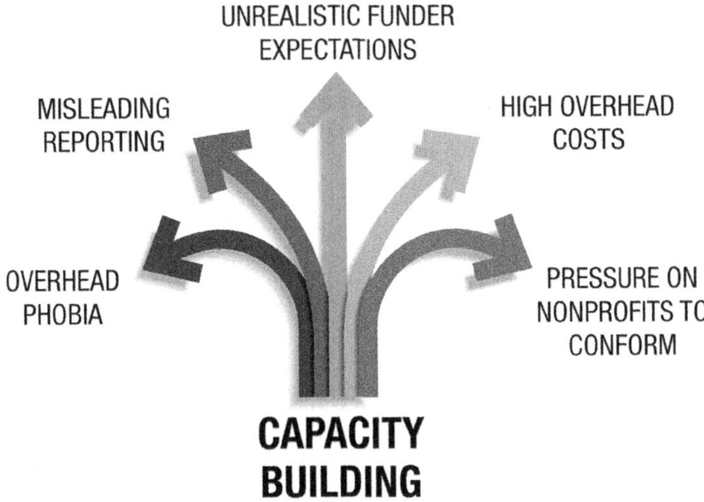

Our attention turns to capacity-building aspects that can hinder positive organizational growth or the offering of business services or products that people want. These are called overhead costs (referred to earlier in the list of capacity-building features). Overhead charges are those elements we cannot attribute to the products or services (programs) but are essential to run a business.

These costs might include rent or mortgage, insurance premiums, equipment, utility costs, and office supplies. For-profit business adds salaries, plus sales and marketing costs (among others, depending on their industry). However, these are the expenditures that businesses are unable to survive without. Overhead serves a very useful purpose.

For-profit organizations often try to discover ways to decrease overhead, as there is some waste that occurs in most companies. Identifying those areas is a start. But proceeding from managing excess can get tricky because you don't want to significantly affect a business's ability to make profits. Finding the right balance can be the solution.

Unfortunately, there is no reasonable formula for overhead that fits every organization. Cutting overhead can be delicate (or brutal) and done on a case-by-case basis. Despite the challenges, it is a sound practice to review the company's overhead regularly and trim where necessary.

Overhead costs can be problematic for business

Overhead costs affect nonprofits differently but are no less of a concern. It comes down to the dynamics observed in the funder relationship. Nonprofits often under-report overhead costs to the people that give them money, because most funders require that overhead be capped at a certain percentage, usually around 15 percent (give or take).

Yet, it is crucial to explore how and why this happens. We need to resolve the reasons it is detrimental to a nonprofit's progress.

Katie Tatham, writing for GuideStar, states, "Overhead expenses are budgeted line items that include rent, administration costs, administrative salaries and bills required to operate." (See end of chapter for resources.)

She goes on to discuss how nonprofits have inadvertently caused the "starvation cycle" and impeded growth by showing less than their actual overhead costs.

Brainstorm the answers to the following questions (be candid!).

1. Has your organization ever under-reported your overhead costs to get money from a funder? In what situation?
2. Have you heard a funder say or request on a grant application that overhead costs have to be capped at a certain percentage?
3. Are you familiar with the term "the starvation cycle" and what it means?

4. Do you pay staff a minimum wage or slightly more because the organization cannot afford additional funds?
5. What would you do if you had adequate amounts of money (or more than enough) for your organization? How would you spend these funds?
6. Do you buy into the idea that not-for-profit means you can only generate enough money to pay for the bottom line and necessary expenses?
7. Everyone who works at or cares about charitable organizations would be wise to watch the TED talk by Dan Pallotta entitled, "The Way We Think About Charity Is Dead Wrong." (See end of chapter for resources.)

He does an eloquent job discussing what he considers to be a necessary change for nonprofits and addresses adapting successful for-profit business approaches. He would also like to revisit and change the overhead problems in nonprofits. Pallotta has identified five issues nonprofits face when they can't invest in their business:

1. Lure top talent away from the for-profit sector.
2. Advertise on the same scale as the for-profit sector.
3. Take risks in pursuit of new customers.
4. Have the same amount of time to find customers as the for-profit sector.
5. Access the stock market to fund their businesses.

As Pallotta states, "The social issues we face, whether they be homelessness or human rights, are large-scale issues. Our organizations are tiny in comparison. Unfortunately, our beliefs around overhead keep them tiny."

Fortunately, the nonprofit field has been examining capacity building linked to changing the limited overhead costs allowed to nonprofits. The small business.chron article noted: "There are no legal requirements for a predetermined maximum of overhead spending for nonprofits. Watchdog groups set maximums and police the spending habits of a nonprofit organization. The financial transparency nonprofits agree to in exchange for tax-exempt status allows watchdog groups, funding organizations, and internal revenue service to identify and hold accountable those organizations that perform poorly in the area of overhead spending." (See end of chapter for resources.)

The logic of watchdog entities looking to see how much nonprofits spend on overhead is well intentioned but problematic. No two nonprofits function alike, even if they are in the same field. To add to this dilemma, everyone calculates operating expenses a bit differently. They can also include various, but not necessarily the same, aspects of their business. As previously noted, the standard or acceptable amount for nonprofit overhead costs has been around 15 percent of an organization's overall operating costs. Most nonprofits cannot honestly include all that is considered administrative and live within those parameters.

In a *GuideStar* blog post, Brian Saber writes: "Constantly harping on a 15% ideal is simplistic and is causing great harm to many wonderful, worthy organizations. Without lots of background information, detailed financials, and an in-depth analysis of an organization's 15%, overhead is meaningless."

And then there's a helpful snippet from a *Bridgespan* blog post on overhead: "Donors tend to reward organizations with the leanest overhead. So nonprofit leaders feel pressure to spend as little as possible on backbone expenses like human resources or I.T. whatever the real cost to their overall effectiveness. This vicious cycle ignores the fact that some overhead is 'good overhead'—the kind that enables an organization to invest in the talent, systems, and training that create a foundation for healthy growth." (See end of chapter for resources.)

I remember speaking with auditors about the yearly tax document (Form 990) required by nonprofits (instead of paying taxes). I asked them how to show our overhead, including fundraising costs.

Although they prepared the document for the Internal Revenue Service, they reported it as what we wanted to display, reminding us about the standard 15 percent overhead. While I am aware that many charities under-report their overhead costs on documents to the IRS and others, it is not technically illegal.

Government standards of applying overhead and what you can deduct often don't match the real costs of running an organization. It leads charities to under-report out of necessity. Unfortunately, along with governments, foundation funders think they are justified in capping overhead, so nonprofits keep turning in the numbers they approve.

Think about overhead costs

- Why is it essential to change the current nonprofit thinking about overhead costs?
- Is there more than one method to calculate your overhead costs?
- Are you finding fundraising costs complicated when you are filling out your 990?
- Have you discovered some of your programs are more expensive to run than others?
- Are overhead costs different across the United States? How are you affected?
- What are some action steps you might take to change this paradigm of capping overhead costs at 15 percent maximum?

The "starvation cycle" is a commentary on nonprofits' misleading reports regarding overhead expenses caused by unrealistic expectations and pressure to conform by some funders. Many in the nonprofit sector believe it has gone too far. Fortunately, the nonprofit world is fighting for equity regarding overhead costs. The field has trained us to think that overhead expenses must be kept low; perhaps we can now be trained to believe otherwise.

In California, Cal Nonprofits is grabbing the tiger by the tail. It is educating nonprofit staff, funders, and influencing policy through its Nonprofit Overhead Project. Its credo is, "It's time to change how we think about nonprofit overhead." The basic thrust of its overhead project includes:

- What is overhead?
- How much is too much overhead?
- How low overhead hurts nonprofits.
- How to get involved.

Capacity building and problems with it affect the foundation of most business. It's time to review or trim overhead costs that impact the business. It's also time that nonprofits should be ready to report a semblance of their true operating costs.

We must end the starvation cycle. To do so, we need to shift our attitudes around nonprofit spending. Dan Pallotta makes the excellent point in his TED talk that "if we truly expect nonprofits to solve society's social ills, then we need to allow nonprofits to have the same advantages big business has."

Potential steps to take to fix low overhead costs

- Look at your approximate real figure for current overhead costs. How did this percentage get figured out?
- Research the issue if needed so you have a clear understanding and talking points on what needs altering. There are great articles online that can inform this research.

- Review organizations like Cal Nonprofits (calnonprofits.org) that are modifying the low overhead percentage rate. Understand the approach and what the takeaways and applications are.
- Discuss overhead costs with other nonprofits. Is there consensus around how to calculate nonprofit operating expenses? Are there some programs that cost more to run? Decide how to advance. Remember, there is strength in numbers.
- Do board members or funders think "overheard cost is an indication of impact"? See Brian Saber's *GuideStar* blog post mentioned earlier in this section on capacity building. Start the conversation with nonprofit directors and board members. Apply strategic thinking.
- Be proactive. Speak with funders to change the starvation cycle.

Funders are amenable to the 15 percent overhead charge since it seems to work. Nonprofits inadvertently feed this requirement by adhering to it and not expressing their anxiety. This type of mindset gives way to the starvation cycle. However, organizations need to make the case with contributors that money for essential infrastructure costs adds value to the cause.

For-profit business is smart to watch their bottom line, but not for the same reasons as nonprofits. Since most businesses are in it for a return on their investment, these enterprises are wise to watch their overhead costs. Their revenue can get eaten up by a little waste here and there that tallies up to be substantial costs that most can't afford.

For-profit ideas on capacity building to put into practice

- Ensure your overhead costs are not causing loss of profits by regularly looking at these expenditures.

- Develop a business plan to start a new business, broaden your business scope, secure funding from investors, or merge with another company.
- Protect your organization from embezzlement by having sound financial management that includes robust internal controls, systematic checks and balances, adequate supervision, and by cultivating trustworthy financial employees.

Nonprofit opportunities for capacity building

- Are you guilty of contributing to the starvation struggle? Be proactive. Convene a phone call or meeting with funders and/or peers that can help you figure out solutions.
- Not being able to afford what people are worth is a travesty and sends the wrong signal. Nonprofits need to look at solutions to having competent employees and paying them equitably.
- Protect your organization from embezzlement by having sound financial management (see for-profit business ideas).

More research on capacity building

- "What Is Capacity Building?" National Council of Nonprofits, https://www.councilofnonprofits.org/tools-resources/what-capacity-building
- "Strengthening Capacity Building in the Nonprofit Sector," Emily Drake and Alex Hildebrand, Learning for Action, 2017, http://learningforaction.com/lfa-blogpost/nonprofit-capacity-building
- "Debunking the 15% Overhead for Good," Brian Saber, *GuideStar* blog, February 2, 2016, https://www.alliancemagazine.org/blog/debunking-the-15-overhead-for-good-2/

- "Nonprofit Overhead Costs: Breaking the Vicious Cycle of Misleading Reporting and the Unrealistic Expectations and Pressure to Conform," William Bedsworth, Ann Goggins Gregory, and Don Howard, *Bridgespan*, April 1, 2008, https://tinyurl.com/2p8br65w
- "How Much Can a Non-Profit Legally Spend on Overhead?" Small Business Chron., https://smallbusiness.chron.com/much-can-nonprofit-legally-spend-overhead-72388.html
- "What Is Overhead Cost and How Do You Calculate It?" FreshBooks, https://www.freshbooks.com/hub/accounting/overhead-cost

Books

- *The Top Twenty Sustainability Strategies for Nonprofits (Nonprofit Toolkit Book 2): Techniques to Ensure Long-term Growth and Sustainability*, Marilyn L. Donnellan. CreateSpace (2018).
- *Nonprofit Capacity Building: A Guide to Self-Directed Capacity Building,* Chukwuemeka Anthony Umeh. CreateSpace (2017).
- *Sustaining Nonprofit Performance: The Case for Capacity Building and Evidence to Support It*, Paul C. Light. Brookings Institution Press (2004).
- *Charity Case: How the Nonprofit Community Can Stand Up for Itself and Really Change the World*, Dan Pallotta. Jossey-Bass (2012).

TED Talk

- "The Way We Think About Charity Is Dead Wrong," Dan Pallotta, TED Talk, March 2013, https://www.ted.com/talks/dan_pallotta_the_way_we_think_about_charity_is_dead_wrong/transcript?language=en

Chapter 16:
THRIVE WITH SUPPORT
Coaching

"Coaching takes a holistic view of the individual: work, values, personal needs and career development are made to work in synergy, not against one another."

British Journal of Administrative Management

Coaching: *Unlocks a person's potential to maximize their performance. Coaching helps them to learn rather than teaching them.*

Internationalcoachingcommunity.com

Executive coaching

Coaching is working one-on-one with a trained professional who functions as a sounding board. The coach can support an individual's work through leadership challenges, assist in managing organizational change, support and help digest feedback, and co-create a plan of support.

This approach ultimately adds value to leadership and the organization. The "right" coach can help transform problems into gifts. As a student of coaching, you must have a desire to learn and grow.

Being in a leadership role in most business is challenging, fast-paced, and a multifaceted job. At a small-to-medium-size company or if you're an entrepreneur, you're supposed to be good at every aspect of running the organization. In the nonprofit world, I read somewhere that most executive directors last an average of five years at the job due to this type of complexity.

Leading a smaller organization can be a demanding job, one that asks for an individual to have expertise in general operational oversight, strategy, management, leadership, fundraising, and boards. This list infers a high level of accountability. Coaching can help enrich the individual's skills to manage the many responsibilities of leadership.

It used to be that in the corporate domain, coaches were hired to help problematic employees out the door. This has not been the case for years. Currently, in our fast-paced world, certified coaches are needed to help develop our potential. They can also help us solve organizational problems.

Coaches are often generalists but can specialize in different areas. The person being coached usually determines what he will use the coach for and how often to work with him. One benefit to the organization can be a more effective leader because coaching has helped with positive performance and behavioral shifts.

Guidance from a pro

I was awarded a two-year fellowship for nonprofit executive directors halfway through my tenure at the organization I founded. The local organization that funded and ran my two-year fellowship is in the business of supporting executive directors in meeting the demands of thought-provoking charitable issues. One of the benefits of my fellowship was being with like-minded individuals. There were a dozen of us from various representations of nonprofit work. Another benefit was to positively impact the nonprofits and people we served.

During the fellowship, we tackled common business themes that included staffing/HR issues, fundraising, budgeting, and auditing. Throughout the two years, we worked with great consultants, coaches, and helpful resources. A highlight for me was getting a coach for a year, which the leadership organization paid for.

My coach, Louise, was so reassuring. She became familiar with my style and the issues I faced. She also knew where my buttons got pushed and how to help me navigate murky waters. She coached me on staying cool at work while everyone around me was losing it. Louise and I had a long-distance relationship since I lived on the West Coast, and she was on the East Coast. Our work together was all done on the phone.

We spoke twice a month for an hour. This was (for me) the right amount of time in between sessions (and we could afford it). It allowed me the time to try out what I had learned from our phone conversations. Coaching with Louise built my leadership skills and positively advanced the nonprofit I ran. It made a difference to have a coach with critical skills to help my personal and institutional development.

Distinctions between coaching and psychotherapy

Psychotherapists	Coaches
1. Psychotherapists are taught how to treat mental illness.	1. Coaches are not trained to treat mental illness.
2. Psychotherapists tend to focus more on healing from the past.	2. The focus of coaching is generally in the future.
3. Psychotherapy is typically covered by insurance because it is seen as treating an illness.	3. Coaching is typically not covered by health insurance because the focus is not on treating an illness.
4. Psychotherapy requires an advanced degree, a state license to practice, a rigorous exam, and many supervised hours of practice.	4. Coaching has a certification program, but not everyone who coaches gets certified. It's not a mandate. It also doesn't have many of the rigorous qualifications that therapy has.
5. Psychotherapists have more restrictions than coaches in where and how they offer services. They have to be licensed in the state they practice. Usually, the psychotherapy is in-house but can be outpatient/ remote.	5. Coaches can work nationally or internationally. Coaching frequently happens over the phone or the internet.

Match the numbers from each category to compare and contrast.

Disclaimer: These differences are broad generalizations and do not apply to all coaches and psychotherapists. Adapted from "5 Differences Between Coaching and Psychotherapy," Jenev Caddell. (See end of chapter for resources.)

It's essential to note that there are substantial differences between coaching and therapy. A coaching relationship is an *inquiry-based partnership*. Its focus is on self-discovery. It helps you discover new strategies and insights into your thought processes and habits. In other words, it gives you an understanding of who you are and helps you determine the options regarding the best way to proceed.

Psychotherapy, on the other hand, is described by the American Psychiatric Association (psychiatry.org) as "talk therapy and a way to help people with a wide variety of mental illnesses and emotional difficulties. Psychotherapy can help eliminate or control troubling symptoms so a person can function better and increase wellbeing and healing."

The coaching relationship is in essence the process of self-discovery that helps us uncover new strategies and insights. It gives us perspective on who we are and helps determine the best course of action. There are currently numerous people offering coaching services; finding the "right" coach at an affordable price can be tricky in the nonprofit world. However, it is worthwhile.

A study about coaching in the nonprofit arena conducted by Compass Point Nonprofit Services in Oakland, California (compasspoint.org), found that coaching "had a profound impact on nonprofit leaders' management and leadership skills, relationships with staff and board members, overall job satisfaction and work-life balance, as well as added confidence and adaptability."

Coaching is not a suitable strategy for every leader or executive. However, when you oversee a business, there aren't many people you can discuss confidential issues with. The saying "it's lonely at the top" can apply to leaders of all ilks. In an established coaching partnership, you can talk about any aspect of your work.

Coaching operates best when you are willing to take responsibility for personal issues and actions, which is to say that it can be an awakening process with its rewards, challenges, and insights.

Think about these issues when you decide to hire a coach

- Do research online about coaching questions, coaches, how to best work with a coach, and so on.
- Speak with colleagues who have worked with coaches before and see if they have any suggestions, cautions, or advice.
- Come up with interview questions (see separate box on the next page).
- What qualities are you looking for in a coach?
- Does the coach possess the appropriate cultural competency?
- Is the coach affordable?
- Does a potential coach have expertise in your nonprofit field of interest? Does it matter?
- Ask yourself: Can I commit to working with the same coach for a year or two?
- Do I need a psychotherapist as opposed to a coach?
- Have I spoken with the coach enough to feel a rapport? Do we share values and priorities?

Interviewing questions for potential coaches

1. What is your experience working in this (my) field?
2. How long have you been in the coaching field?
3. Do you work from a clear methodology? (Are you a match with this methodology?)
4. What is your expertise with the leadership challenges I am facing?
5. How do you instill appropriate boundaries if it seems like we are drifting toward therapy and deeply personal issues?
6. Do you have certification from a (reputable) coaching organization?
7. Is it okay to blow off steam when I've had a tough couple of weeks? Or are there other ways you want me to frame my concerns?
8. What are your coaching fees? Do you charge by the hour, a grouping of sessions, or something else? Will you negotiate?
9. Is there a standard length of time you work with someone?
10. Add your questions here!

Encouraging your key employees to get coaching is a great way to show support for leadership in a business. It is essential to know that a genuine, caring, and fruitful discussion can make a significant difference. Coaching can help with work-life balance and overall job satisfaction. It can be a powerful solution to difficulties in the workplace.

The caution with coaching would be to not engage with a coach to fix psychological problems. That's not her/his job. A coach with plenty of experience has appropriate boundaries.

For-profit coaching ideas to put into practice

- If you are running a business, consider hiring a coach for moving you forward with the issues you're facing including wanting to make more money.
- Remember that there are major differences between a psychotherapist and a coach. Know what kind of development and issues a coach is appropriate for.
- Use a coach who has the expertise in the area where you need the most support.

Nonprofit coaching opportunities

- Give credence to leadership coaching in your organization because it is a worthy and supportive investment.
- While it's vital to stay within the budget constraints in any organization, having a professional give expert support to a key employee is worth its weight in gold.
- It is mandatory that anyone who is going to be coached has the desire to learn and grow or it will be a waste of time and money.

More research on coaching

- "5 Differences Between Coaching and Psychotherapy," Jenev Caddell, September 17, 2020, https://www.verywellmind.com/should-i-work-with-a-psychotherapist-or-coach-2337587.
- "Top 10 Questions About Nonprofit Leadership Coaching," Nonprofit Coach, https://nonprofitcoach.com/leadership-coaching-questions/.

- "Leadership Coaching," https://www.501commons.org/services/coaching-and-executive-advising/coaching.
- Center for Nonprofit Coaching, https://centerfornonprofitcoaching.org/
- NonprofitCoach, https://nonprofitcoach.com/
- "Hiring a Coach: Is It Right for You?" Nicki Roth, The Bridgespan Group, https://www.bridgespan.org/bridgespan/Images/articles/hiring-a-coach-is-it-right-for-you/hiring-a-coach-is-it-right-for-you.pdf.

Books

- *Fierce Conversations, Achieving Success at Work and in Life, One Conversation at a Time*, Susan Scott. Berkley (2004).
- *Coaching Mindset: How to Use Personal Coaching Skills to Reach Your Goals*, Claire Moody. Independently published (2020).
- *Coaching for Performance, 5th Edition: The Principles and Practice of Coaching and Leadership, 25th Anniversary Edition*, John Whitmore. Nicholas Brealey (2017).
- *Coaching Skills for Nonprofit Managers and Leaders: Developing People to Achieve Your Mission*, Judith Wilson and Michelle Gislason. Jossey-Bass (2009).
- *Coaching for Transformation: Pathways to Ignite Personal & Social Change*, Martha Lasley, Virginia Kellogg, Richard Michaels, and Sharon Brown. Discover Press (2015).

Chapter 17:
PEOPLE AT THE TOP
Board of Directors

"You are not here merely to make a living. You are here to enable the world to live more amply with greater vision, with a finer spirit of help and achievement. You are here to enrich the world, and you impoverish yourself if you forget the errand."

Woodrow Wilson

Board of Directors: *A group of people who manage or direct a company or organization.*

Merriam-Webster Dictionary

Board of directors

This chapter is all about the unique role that the board of directors (trustees) plays in the life of a corporation, including nonprofits. The trustees make up the governing body that has legal and fiduciary responsibilities for the business.

In conjunction with these duties, boards are tasked with providing oversight to the organization, engaging in and setting strategic policy, protecting the mission, purpose, or values, and often functioning as positive representatives outside the boardroom. A business that is a legal corporation is required to have a board of directors.

The similarities and distinctions among for-profit and nonprofit boards

The essential duties of boards of both types of business overlap in crucial ways. These include the monitoring of legal and fiduciary obligations, offering strategic direction, and ensuring the protection of assets (among other roles). With modifications as required, the material contained in this chapter can apply to most boards.

However, for-profit business boards are different from nonprofit boards. The biggest variance is that for-profit boards have stakeholders or owners and consider how to maximize profits.

The for-profit board is then responsible for protecting shareholders' or owners' investments and revenues, establishing policies for the company, and providing oversight. The bigger challenge for-profit boards lies with an interesting dilemma: Do they protect stakeholders' interests or do they move the business toward a more just and responsible outlook? Hopefully they will figure out how to do both.

Nonprofit boards have another type of stakeholder: the people they serve (encompassing funders as required). They often "make money" through fundraising, and they review financials and support funding through individuals, foundations, the government, and other approaches to support their services and programs.

Nonprofit boards also provide oversight, are mission driven, and act as fundraisers and ambassadors for the organization in the community.

Are boards problematic?

Boards seem central to a well-run organization. However, too many boards, no matter what business they are in, fall into the category of not fulfilling their purpose or understanding their role. There is also a level of frustration and misunderstanding between boards and staff at the organizations they help.

I will go into detail about what the evidence shows, and what I've experienced related to boards. There are challenges for both board members and staff; I explain why I think these and other problems occur.

Each of the following phrases I have heard, read, and/or discussed with colleagues:

- The board of directors is a great addition to our landscape.
- Boards are a ton of work for the staff.
- Boards have no intrinsic value.
- Boards are an extension of the work we do at our organizations—we couldn't live without them.
- Boards are just paint-by-number, then you are supposed to do this, then you are supposed to do that.
- Boards are a mixed bag.
- Forget about boards and fundraising.
- Even though I was in a prime leadership position and truly loved the work, I got out of the field because of the difficulty of managing the board.

While many boards are well intentioned, they need to consider how their service can add practically and conceptually to a mission *or* the bottom line of making a profit. I believe the structure of boards, especially at nonprofits, is a big part of the problem. The best way to put it is that boards, and the organizations they are providing oversight for, are a very complicated paradigm.

A board story to examine

Imagine there was a new board volunteer named Anthony. He was asked, along with fellow members, to oversee a charitable organization. Anthony felt he could fulfill the daunting task of ensuring that the nonprofit was legally and financially responsible.

The board job description stated that it had to offer general oversight to the organization. Additionally, Anthony agreed to be an ambassador in the broader community, give fundraising a go, serve on a committee that met monthly, and attend board meetings (among other crucial duties).

Anthony was committed and looked forward to the volunteer challenge. He had spent twenty years in for-profit financial institutions and respected the charitable organization's mission to provide low-income, multicultural families with needed housing services.

After a few months, Anthony noted that *none* of the other board members were doing any fundraising. To add to his confusion, there was a board development committee whose task was to raise money for the organization. In the meantime, Anthony noticed that a few dedicated staff members were going crazy trying to procure money for the nonprofit.

It was okay because he didn't know how to fundraise or where to begin. Anthony also detected politics between a key staffer and board members. It seemed boundaries between the two entities were not delineated, and a lot of "toe-stepping" occurred.

From what he could tell, it had turned into a "we [board] vs. them [staff]" situation. To make matters more challenging, the board had concerns about Larry, who was the chief executive officer. To some of the board, he appeared to be hiding something.

This caused even more friction and division between the two key bodies of the organization. Regrettably, the board members became split in their loyalties. One group of members was loyal to the board, and the second was loyal to the employees.

It was the power struggle between the staff and the board that got to Anthony the most. He wasn't sure that Larry was hiding anything. He only interacted with him twice a month at meetings and didn't think there were problems. At least the financials didn't show any.

It seemed like the rest of the staff was working hard and doing their job. Anthony thought the divisiveness came from ineffective communication between staff and the board. People just weren't listening to each other.

The other element in play was whether the board was trying to be in control or if they were just providing oversight. Anthony found himself in a confusing dilemma. He was torn and didn't want to take sides.

Anthony resigned after a little less than a year into his three-year tenure. He told other board members he had "stress at the job and home life and couldn't take on more pressure." He didn't get into substantive reasons for his resignation. After all, he was a volunteer and didn't feel he could bring about a significant difference anyway.

Anthony walked away, still wishing that he could have made positive changes for the organization. Instead, he left with concern for the well-being of the nonprofit. He wasn't sure it could withstand this kind of internal politics and maintain its integrity.

What would you do?

- What could be done about the divisiveness between board and staff if you were the board chair? Executive director?
- How might you have handled things differently if you were the board member who resigned?
- How could you have handled communication issues with the board if you were the chair or the chief executive?
- In a leadership role either with staff or board, how do you keep a negative situation from escalating without the risk of creating isolation or more "bad blood"?
- As a board member willing to fundraise, how might you rectify the fundraising situation with the rest of the board?
- How do you keep good people from leaving the board when there are problems?
- In a board or staff leadership role, how could you start a conversation about power without pointing fingers or making people feel judged or blamed?

A lack of job clarity on boards

Too many board members don't really understand their roles and responsibilities, according to BoardSource.org. "This lack of understanding of what is—and is not—a part of the board's essential roles, can lead to a whole host of dysfunctions, such as micromanagement, rogue decision-making, lack of engagement, and more." (See end of chapter for resources.)

An absence of definitiveness about a board member's job description can be problematic. A misperception about how oversight works can lend itself to blurred boundaries and role confusion. How does a board member execute primary responsibilities without it becoming difficult for the organization?

Ideally, a board has an objective view of the organization's functioning. It can identify where potential strengths and weaknesses lie. However, if the board lacks knowledge or insight in any significant area regarding its role, or the actual business it is governing, the enterprise is ripe for challenges. Boards may only possess a basic knowledge of the organization's processes, operations, programs, products, and/or structure.

The literature clearly states that a board provides legal and fiduciary oversight, advances the mission/values, and manages its resources. Yet it doesn't necessarily say how they should do this. People interpret their board functions in a variety of ways.

Boards lack basic knowledge about the implementation of duties

- Boards have inadequate training in their essential roles and responsibilities.
- Board members are not clear regarding their expectations.
- Boards don't know what it means to provide oversight. Overseeing an organization is not explained or detailed out.
- The board chair does not have appropriate leadership skills. Training in this role is not offered by the organization.
- Board members don't know the organization's systems (e.g., operations, processes, programs, and structures). The staff hasn't been involved or asked to give presentations to help board members understand the organization.
- The board role is too large and overwhelming. Members don't have the time, energy, or resources to tackle their functions.

- There are duties mentioned, like fundraising in the nonprofit sector, that only a select few like to perform. Most boards do not fundraise.

A unified vision goes a long way in helping boards understand the work that lies ahead. The leadership of boards needs to provide direction on roles. Also, it requires repetition since it's often fundamental issues that "trip up" boards.

According to the *Nonprofit Quarterly*, "The past twenty years have seen the steady growth of training programs, consulting practices, academic research, and guidebooks aimed at improving the performance of nonprofit boards. This development reflects both hopes and doubts about the nonprofit board. On the one hand, boards are touted as a decisive force for ensuring the accountability of nonprofit organizations. On the other hand, the board is widely regarded as a problematic institution." (See end of chapter for resources).

Specific board duties

The list in the box contains basic board duties. Add or subtract functions depending on your board.

Duties that boards perform

1. Responsible for legal and fiduciary obligations, including accountability for the organization.
2. Ongoing board development to review roles and duties.
3. Regularly apply a strategic focus and direction, and ensure effective organizational planning.
4. Ensure adequate resources.
5. Enhance the organization's image and culture.

6. Subscribe to and be aware of the organization's bylaws.
7. Act as ambassadors and positive advocates in the community.
8. Advance the mission or purpose of the organization.
9. Fundraise on behalf of the nonprofit.
10. Hire/fire the executive director.

*Nonprofits have accountability for items 1–10.
For-profit organizations are engaged in items 1–6.

This inventory of board responsibilities is compiled from numerous websites, including nationalcouncilofnonprofits.org, boardsource.org, nonprofitquarterly.org, proplenonprofits.org, and boardeffect.com.

Please remember we are all experiencing the human condition differently. No one is flawless. There will be problems to solve, no matter how hard you try to follow best practices. Minimize these complications and give the benefit of the doubt to people in service to the organization. In all these pages, it is empowerment and respect we are after. These are true values we need to see a lot more of in most business environments.

The lawful accountability of boards

The legal responsibilities of boards are the duties of care, loyalty, and obedience. This is a theoretical approach to the allowed duties that boards perform at organizations, whether they be for-profits or nonprofits.

It is helpful to break down the philosophy and get to the actual meaning of the obligations of boards since it is key to understanding why boards are significant. These duties are also referred to as fiduciary responsibilities. Once understood, it helps the concept to come alive and leave some of the dryness aside.

What is a fiduciary? According to Investopedia, "A fiduciary is a person or an organization that acts on behalf of another person or persons to manage assets. Essentially, a fiduciary owes to that other entity the duties of good faith and trust." (See end of chapter for resources.)

To put it in layman's terms, when a nonprofit board is a fiduciary, it means the board acts honorably and in the best interest of the organization. Board fiduciaries are asked to put the organization's interests before their own. A fiduciary responsibility is most often linked to financials but includes all of an organization's resources.

The legal obligations of boards are broken down into three conceptual categories called duty of care, loyalty, and obedience. There are many interpretations of these formalized obligations. These legal mandates for boards are quoted from "Board Roles and Responsibilities" by the National Council of Nonprofits. (See end of chapter for resources.) I have added an interpretation of what it means after the quote.

Duty of Care: *Take care of the business by ensuring prudent use of all assets, including facilities, people, and goodwill.*

Duty of care means board members must exercise reasonable care when making decisions on behalf of the organization. It speaks to strategic thinking and planning. Boards also provide general oversight of the nonprofit's activities.

Duty of Loyalty: *Ensure that the company's activities and transactions are, first and foremost, advancing its mission. Recognize and disclose conflicts of interest; make decisions that are in the best interest of the corporation, not in the best interest of the individual board member.*

The duty of loyalty refers to each board member publicly disclosing any conflicts of interest. Additionally, it means not using board service as a means of personal or commercial gain. It is an act of trustworthiness. Board members sign a conflict-of-interest agreement. Conflict-of-interest policies are available free of charge online.

Duty of Obedience: *Ensure that the enterprise obeys applicable laws and regulations, follows its bylaws, and adheres to its stated corporate purposes and mission.*

The duty of obedience requires board members not to engage in any illegal or unauthorized activities. It mandates that the organization is abiding by all applicable laws and regulations. It is faithful to the organization's mission and/or values.

Understand that the three duties of care, loyalty, and obedience are required by law. They are the broad brushstrokes that paint a picture of board duties at any corporation. Not understanding these duties doesn't release one from the legal issues that could follow.

Comprehending and then performing these duties can lead to a more participatory culture. The board meetings can become an effective platform for members to discuss and make decisions about issues that the business is facing.

How well is your board functioning?

The first list describes the ideal way a board can function. The second list documents potential board problems. To assess how well your board is functioning, have people go through these lists, giving their boards pluses/minuses or leaving it blank. Then add up each column and see which one has the most. Decide on a plan of action from here.

Leaning more toward pluses

The board does a successful job of performing its legal and fiduciary responsibilities.

The board is implementing an ongoing strategic thinking process that they track.

Diversity is sought after and appreciated on the board.

New board members have ongoing and comprehensive training on the duties and roles.

The board understands governance and uses its power wisely.

The board shares its power appropriately with the staff's chief executive.

The board serves as ambassadors in the community.

The nonprofit board reviews the chief executive each year.

The board annually and honestly evaluates itself.

Add to this list as appropriate.

Leaning more toward minuses

The board members don't understand its roles and what they are supposed to be doing for the business.

The board doesn't know what it means to provide oversight, so it doesn't do it.

The board chair does not provide suitable leadership.

The board does not annually or regularly review the chief executive's performance.

The board wants to see a strategic plan, but doesn't necessarily want to be involved in creating it.

The board doesn't fundraise.

New board members lack proper role training.

The board does not enforce term limits.

The board does not have appropriate boundaries with staff

Add to this list as appropriate.

Leaning more toward pluses	Leaning more toward minuses
• The board does a successful job of performing its legal and fiduciary responsibilities.	• The board members don't understand their roles and what they are supposed to be doing for the business.
• The board is implementing an ongoing strategic thinking process that they track.	• The board doesn't know what it means to provide oversight, so it doesn't do it.
• Diversity is sought after and appreciated on the board.	• The board chair does not provide suitable leadership.
• New board members have ongoing and comprehensive training on the duties and roles.	• The board does not annually or regularly review the chief executive's performance.
• The board understands governance and uses its power wisely.	• The board wants to see a strategic plan but, doesn't necessarily want to be involved in creating it
• The board shares its power appropriately with the staff's chief executive.	• The board doesn't fundraise.
• The board members serve as ambassadors in the community.	• New board members lack proper role training.
• The nonprofit board reviews the chief executive each year.	• The board does not enforce term limits.
• The board annually and honestly evaluates itself.	• The board does not have appropriate boundaries with staff.
Add to this list as appropriate.	*Add to this list as appropriate.*

Think about how well the board is doing with the exercise of pluses and minuses.

See which side has a longer list of pluses or minuses. Which carries more "weight" and why?

What is the board doing well? Have you celebrated their accomplishments?

What practices on the board can be changed or eliminated? What can be enhanced?

What is a problem area that surfaced that you know the board can work on?

Can you or someone else move the board to a more productive place?

Can trainings help the board understand their roles?

The three stages in a board's life cycle

Of all the information out there about boards, I found the concept of the three stages in a board's life cycle to be the easiest to understand and apply. Board service and how one executes it can be vital to an organization. As comprehension dawns on board members regarding their job duties, they come to understand the significant work that needs to happen moving forward. Therefore, it becomes helpful to know where a board is in its progression.

There are three stages of nonprofit board development that have been identified by Karl Mathiasen III. These phases include an *organizing or founding board*, a *governing board*, and an *institutional board*. (See end of chapter for resources.) These stages refer to charitable organization boards. Yet, it is essential for all business to understand these phases, since there is critical information to be learned from them.

Stage 1-A) Founding board

An organizing or founding board is often small and committed. During this period, the board doesn't generally perform tasks or take on significant fundraising roles. This stage is also described as the cheerleading board since board members are on the sidelines, cheering their leader on, saying, "I know you can do it." Board committees don't tend to be formed at this stage of development.

In effect, they want the leader and a small staff to succeed but might not be willing to roll up their sleeves and dig in. The board is composed of people the leader knows well and who have a strong commitment to his or her vision. They advise, encourage, and offer a sounding board. It is called the founding (or following) board because they follow the leaders who started the nonprofit.

I enlisted school personnel for the first board for the organization that I ran. These lovely individuals were happy to serve, but I wasn't sure how much work they wanted to do. One of the board volunteers talked regularly about how anxious he was to get to his planned kitchen remodel.

The stages of board development that rely on the executive director are usually considered a "following board." It can be appropriate in many cases to stay this way for as long as it takes. To go to the next stage, which is a governing board, takes a sizeable paradigm shift and a lot of work.

Stage 1-B) Organizing board

This is also considered a first stage of board development. An organizing board relates to the founders of the organization who usually run it. They can be like-minded members who have a strong sense of ownership. Yet, it can quickly turn into a challenge once the organization hires employees. The transition to working with staff can be difficult. And even after it happens, employees may have to be patient before they are trusted.

After this stage, there is a transition to a governing board. This happens when the founder/executive director realizes that he needs help managing an increasingly complex organization and that the board must become more engaged. Boards in the transition stage start feeling the strain of being tasked to do more. The board is reluctant to change its role.

Stage 2. Middle stage: Governing board or managing board

The middle stage is when the board moves from relative inactivity and cheerleading to the gradual assumption of the organization's governance. The board gets active in the organization's work, oversees its finances, and is accountable for its integrity. Committees become essential to effective board functioning, and fundraising becomes more of a responsibility than an option.

Board governance is the period of work most often used to describe boards. If board members are willing to work hard to provide the oversight specified in their job descriptions and meet all of their fiduciary responsibilities, including fundraising, it can be an appropriate progression (although this is not often the case).

The stages of board development are essential to look at and discuss before a nonprofit decides if it wants to move to the next phase of its evolution. It can allow for intelligent, fruitful discussions with all parties it impacts. It's a nonjudgmental approach and shows a natural progression of growth. This mindful process, in the long run, can prove to be less stressful.

Stage 3: The mature stage: Institutional board

This phase primarily affects large nonprofits that have been around for a long time. They are often prestigious organizations. They recruit board members who can give or open doors to funders and donors. This type of board pays attention to major organizational issues and concerns.

The mature stage of a board is not one that I have personally experienced. Yet, I have seen charitable organizations locally and nationally fit the description. Many small to mid-size nonprofits stay in the first two stages of board development. "If it's not broken, don't fix it," as the saying goes. It is not necessary to move to the mature stage of board growth unless it fits the organization's evolution.

The next stage up of board development should be undertaken only if the trustees and staff can take on the additional responsibilities and make that paradigm shift. For instance, the mature stage of governance has complex duties and expectations associated with it. The board role could get much more demanding than that of a founding board. Stay at the founding board stage if that's your comfort zone. There is no one to say you must move along the continuum of board development.

Allow the timing of moving from one board stage to another to be optimum. Considerable planning needs to be undertaken when you move to another board development stage. Use a conscious and thoughtful process. Apply strategic thinking and have the board and staff design a plan with a timeline.

I find this material to be very enlightening. When I first became an executive director, this concept of board stages was all the rage. I believe it remains of substantial value to the field, with the caveats being numerous boards can defy categorization because there are exceptions to the rules.

My early board experiences

I first served as an executive director on a board in 1996. I recruited five school-related personnel to board positions. That relationship lasted just shy of two years. We succeeded in acquiring the 501(c)(3) designation from the IRS and our certificate of incorporation from the State of California. We also executed the initial strategic plan that created our vision and mission statements.

That association ended when our fiscal guy, Rex, made another (in a series of plenty) disparaging comment about the board's minimum involvement in fundraising. To this fledgling board, this was the straw that broke the camel's back. Everyone quit within a few days, except for me and one other brave soul.

Rex felt so terrible about his unfortunate comments that he recruited our next board chair. Jane stayed with us for fifteen years. She was knowledgeable about how to run nonprofits and be on boards. In the many years that she was with us, she single-handedly brought in millions of dollars.

Jane achieved this remarkable act of fundraising through knowing people at foundations that continued to give the organization money for long periods. She also mentored me since she knew more about running nonprofits than I did. Additionally, Jane helped us buy our first building. She believed wholeheartedly in our purpose, the community, and our services.

Jane has four grown children. Many years ago, she brought her little girl Alice to the nonprofit. About three at the time, Alice was adorable and quite precocious. She came running over to her mom as she ran out of one of the playrooms and said enthusiastically, "Mommy, Mommy, they have toys just like the ones at our house!" Well, they were *their* donated toys, but with big grins on our faces, we didn't tell her that.

Under Jane's tutelage, we ran fundraisers that were 100 percent put on by the board. They were super but netted hardly any money. Jane told me repeatedly during her last three years as board chair that she wanted to get off the board. Simultaneous to this conversation with Jane, I thought we were ready for the next stage of the board, which was governance, since we needed more help. That was in 2012. We were preparing for our 2013 strategic plan, and creating a governing board was one of the important ideas we had put out there.

Test your board knowledge

True or False

1. Nonprofit board members do not really need to fundraise. Certain conditions apply that let boards off the hook: If they aren't fundraisers by nature, don't have the expertise, or know people that have money.

   Answer: False. While boards may understand the need to fundraise, the majority do not. Boards need to help with the fundraising. Francis Ostrower's groundbreaking study of five thousand nonprofit organizations *found that only 29 percent of boards are active in fundraising.*

   The lack of board fundraising is a genuine problem because boards are fiscally responsible for an organization, meaning they oversee all of the regular financials and audits. They need to talk about and really support fundraising, even if they bring in small amounts of money. Until this requirement is changed, boards need to help in fundraising.

2. A board's composition impacts how it leads.

   Answer: True. A board's composition does indeed impact how it leads. A BoardSource research report titled "Leading with Intent: 2017 National Index of Nonprofit Board Practice" highlights in depth the link between the effectiveness of a solid board composition to how it leads.

   I would caution that board membership is often in flux, so just when you think you have the ideal structure, it can change.

Remember that when you are putting together a board composition chart, record what you need boards to do as opposed to just their skills.

3. Board members intuitively know how to govern, especially if they have well-crafted job and committee descriptions.
   Answer: False. We have to teach people how to be effective governors on boards. The training should be ongoing. It is so much more than just wearing a label that says, "we are governors." Members need to understand their roles and the organization intimately and grasp where the nonprofit needs the most support.
   At the same time, the chair should be working closely with board members to see that they are responsible for the duties they signed up to perform. Having well-thought-out board and committee descriptions is not adequate to demonstrate how effective governance works.
4. Board members like to focus on accountability, making it a compelling purpose.
   Answer: True and False. Boards like to have accountability for organizations. Yet, the literature on nonprofit boards has shown that "accountability is not enough to sustain interest, let alone membership. Some of the important functions that boards must perform, such as monitoring and oversight, are not very engaging to board members and are not why many people join a board."
5. When you study the stages of board development, and the organization you know is still a founding board ten years later, it's okay not to be a governing board.
   Answer: True. An organization can stay at its current stage of board development if it is working. Boards don't mature at the same rate. Some boards are great just the way they are and do not need to change their developmental stage.

Self-perpetuating behaviours

- Poor communications between staff and board leadership
- Board demonstrates power over staff, lack of trust between the two entities
- Board members are the experts, not staff
- Board role confusion
- Poor boundaries between board and staff
- Board controls without responsibility
- Lack of equality between the CEO and the board chair and board

Power imbalances

I am committed to a collective vision of the world that business expertise can bring. However, when it comes to boards of directors, I have repeatedly seen or experienced top-down or power-over models that many boards are encouraged to follow. The business world and nonprofit specialists accept governance with little exception.

I have witnessed numerous uninformed board decisions made in the name of following ordained "policies" from so-called "experts." Also, boards can "cherry-pick" what they want to do or don't want to do (e.g., we're not a fundraising board), and there is no one to tell them "no." Unfortunately, this can lead to obvious disregard for what is best for the organization.

The question of who boards are responsible and accountable to needs to be answered. Right now, they can do what they think is best for the organization, even if the staff disagrees with their decision. Role confusion is widespread in boards, yet they are empowered to make determinations for the business that can have far-reaching negative consequences.

As humans, we all have our weak points. Why, then, are trustees' motives unquestioned and their work unopposed? And if things don't go well with board decisions, often staff or others are seen as the problem. The board of directors can be out of touch with the realities at hand, especially since they are doing most of their monitoring remotely and not day-to-day.

Power with little accountability for outcomes can become irresponsibility and tyranny.

Boards can stay in a bubble and justify board agreements to an agency with dubious claims about the greater good. There is a lack of checks and balances for board members.

Boards appear to have an underlying structural problem. I am not contesting the need for corporate oversight. It can be useful. But what happens when boards go unchecked? Problems can ensue, including a board chair or a board member impeding the progress of an organization.

The very essence of nonprofit formation is to create altruism, and to make the world a better place. I have spoken at length in the second chapter about empowerment. I explain why it's so vital that every business staff and board member is grounded in and empowering each other. It's the initial step in agreeing to make companies a more caring place to do the work that gives optimism and purpose to others.

A cautionary board tale

It was 2013, and I remember recruiting new members for the board, which remained a constant throughout my nonprofit career. A man we will call Samuel captured my attention.

He attended a prestigious higher education institution to secure an advanced degree. He was smart, fun, energetic, and had served on boards before. In my mind, he was the perfect board chair. In 2014, I asked him to become the chair.

By 2015, he began to sink his teeth into the role. He told me around the same time that the board was a governing board and they had the right to take charge. Simultaneously, something else was happening. He and others on the board had a poor response to my leadership. During a board meeting, without any prior communication to me, he asked me to leave right after the midpoint, while they continued to engage.

The board decided to go into a closed session without staff. This can be a standard procedure. However, we hadn't established a precedent for it. I honestly didn't understand what was happening. I presumed they wanted to discuss how I carried out my duties, but there was no prior indication that this was what was occurring.

Afterwards, I called a longtime board member I considered to be a friend and asked what had gone on in the closed session. His hostile answer surprised me. He said that I was challenging to work with, antagonistic toward board members, and had other difficult behaviors. The real kicker was that I had "too much power." These were completely revelatory and yet alarming statements to hear!

I believe the board was trying to remedy my supposed management issues without speaking to me. They had decided they were a governing board without letting me know. Unfortunately, the trustees' disapproval toward me didn't stop. The lack of direct communication with the board deteriorated as their suspicions of my "unsatisfactory" performance intensified.

Samuel was suggestive in his approach and had swayed the board to thinking I was consistently inappropriate with others. While they were asking tough questions about my performance to each other, they weren't asking these unpleasant questions to me directly.

Despite numerous interventions, including working with expensive board consultants, nothing could reestablish trust or salvage a positive working relationship. I also added fuel to the flames by wanting to change my retirement date.

In the 2013 strategic plan, my optimistic exit time had been projected for December 2018. I truly wanted to retire but I had no idea when that could happen. So, I picked a random date in what seemed like a remote future for the strategy write-up.

However, in the meantime, there had been enormous mitigating circumstances. We bought a five-thousand-square-foot building in May 2015 for our branch office. It desperately needed extensive renovations and over two million dollars of funding to make it happen. I felt responsible since I was told repeatedly (by members of the board) that they weren't fundraisers.

I thought I had communicated adequately to the board about the reasons I needed to defer my departure time until a later date. Yet, two or three board members were angered by my decision. Despite their reservations, I decided to stay to finish the branch office's expansion.

Think about this cautionary board story

Where do the cautions lie in this story?

- Could the communications between the executive director (ED) and the board be mended?
- In these circumstances, what would you have done if you were the ED?
- What could you have done if you were part of the board of directors?
- Why were tough questions not being asked by either the board or the ED?
- Why was the closed session described in the story problematic for the executive director and ultimately the board?
- How would you have handled the alleged performance issues with the ED?
- What were the biggest board/staff lessons that came out of this scenario?

The board of directors continues to be an essential part of business. I am not saying do away with boards. Companies need the oversight, accountability, and all the duties trustees perform. However, there seem to be some genuine problems on boards. These challenging behaviors have been the subject of extensive research and many pricey board consultants.

I understand that boards can be in charge and provide oversight. Yet it is the governing board's fundamental structure and duties that create an unequal distribution of power. Subsequently, staff can be seen as the lesser of the two bodies. Boards oversee a nonprofit, yet they don't often know the operations, services, and what makes an organization tick.

They get muddled about their roles and the boundaries between them and staff, don't think they have to fundraise, and are not necessarily reflective of the diversity of the participants. Yet, they hold authority and use it.

We need a shift from top-down hierarchies to working together innovatively as a balanced team for the organization's betterment. I propose that we gradually transform the concept of board of directors. In Chapter 18, "Innovative Potentials," I offer imaginative solutions to basic thorny board issues mentioned herein.

For-profit board ideas to put into practice

- Strategy is key. Ensure the board is moving in the right direction with regular time for strategic thinking.
- The board chair needs to manage the board of directors and consistently educate and review what their roles are. Additionally, the chair must establish the reason they are currently needed for the business.
- Implement a buddy system for new board members. Pair experienced, willing board members with new ones and establish ground rules for preferred actions.

Nonprofit board opportunities

- Broaden your definition of fiduciary to include "all resources" so the board knows they are overseeing and protecting the whole organization.
- As key staff, work with the board chair to establish and model an appropriate working partnership. You want it to filter through to the rest of the board and staff.
- The board and chief executive should review the *Three Stages in a Board's Life Cycle* to ensure the board is in the right phase of its development.

More research on boards of directors

- Fundamental topics of nonprofit board service, BoardSource.org, https://boardsource.org/fundamental-topics-of-nonprofit-board-service/roles-responsibilities/
- Problem boards or board problems, Winter 2012, *Nonprofit Quarterly,* https: https://store.nonprofitquarterly.org/products/problem-boards-or-board-problem
- National Council of Nonprofits. Board Roles and Responsibilities, https://www.councilofnonprofits.org|tools-resources|board-roles-and-responsibilites
- BoardSource, Three Stages in a Nonprofit Boards Lifecycle https://boardsource.org/three-stages-nonprofit-board-lifecycle/
- *Nonprofit Quarterly*, Nonprofit Governance, https://nonprofitquarterly.org/welcome-to-emerging-forms-of-nonprofit-governance
- "A Guide to the Big Ideas and Debates in Corporate Governance," Lynn S. Paine and Suraj Srinivasan, *Harvard Business Review*, October 14, 2019, https://hbr.org/2019/10/a-guide-to-the-big-ideas-and-debates-in-corporate-governance

- The Corporate Board, https://corporateboard.com.
- Board Support Program for Nonprofit Organizations, BoardSource, https://boardsource.org/board-support/membership/board-support-nonprofits/
- "Nonprofit Board Responsibilities: The Basics," Herrington J. Bryce, *Nonprofit Quarterly*, August 21, 2017, https://nonprofitquarterly.org/nonprofit-board-governance-responsibilities-basic-guide/
- "Boards in the Time of Coronavirus," Martin Hirt, Celia Huber, Frithjof Lund, and Nina Spielmann, McKinsey & Company, https://www.mckinsey.com/business-functions/strategy-and-corporate-finance/our-insights/boards-in-the-time-of-coronavirus
- "Ten Basic Responsibilities of Nonprofits," Richard T. Ingram, InPhilanthrophy.org, https://www.inphilanthropy.org/sites/default/files/resources/Ten%20Basic%20Responsibilities%20of%20Nonprofit%20Boards-Natl%20Center%20NP%20Boards.pdf

Books on board of directors

- *The Nonprofit Board Answer Book: A Practical Guide for Board Members and Chief Executives, 3rd edition.* Jossey-Bass (2011).
- *Sarbanes-Oxley and the Board of Directors: Techniques and Best Practices for Corporate Governance* Scott Green. John Wiley & Sons (2005).
- *Fix This Next, Make the Vital Change That Will Level Up Your Business,* Mike Michalowic. Penguin (2020).
- *Governance as Leadership: Reframing the Work of a Nonprofit Board*, Barbara E. Taylor, Richard Chait, and William P. Ryan. John Wiley & Sons (2004).

- *Effective Leadership for Nonprofit Organizations: How Executive Directors and Boards Work Together*, Thomas Wolf. Allworth (2014).
- "Leadership, Governance and the Work of the Board," David O. Renz, in *The Jossey-Bass Handbook of Nonprofit Leadership and Management*, 4th edition, David O. Renz and Associates. Jossey-Bass (2016).

Chapter 18: INNOVATIVE POTENTIALS

Board of Directors Solutions

"There's a way to do it better—find it."

Thomas Edison

Board of Directors Problems: *A dysfunctional board of directors has the ability to cause multiple headaches for your business or organization. Not only will a dysfunctional board of directors often fail to make decisions that are in the best interest of the organization, but its dysfunction also has the potential to move outside the confines of the boardroom, causing negative publicity.*

smallbusiness.chron.com

Unique solutions for board issues

What follows in this chapter are potential solutions for challenges facing boards. The hope is that these suggestions can support trustees to become more equity minded, understanding, and purposeful about executing their roles. Often boards get mired in problems that don't further the organization.

It is collectively time to look at a new paradigm, with values such as respect, equality, and justice being front and center. Organizations thrive because both board and staff understand what's at stake and are willing to work together. Fundamental to this idea is that the world of business undergoes a transformation regarding the power it's given to boards.

Think about these essential board questions

1. Are the trustees regularly reviewing the roles and the power they are given?
2. Is the board using their authority appropriately? According to whom?
3. In what manner is the assistance from the board helping the organization they're serving?
4. Is the board work benefiting staff? The organization? How so?

What follows is a collection of board remedies. Some are from business sources, while others are culled from the problems I have witnessed, heard, or read about. I know for a fact that boards get really confused by their roles. Clarifying the board obligations is a good place to start.

Practical remedies from *Leading with Intent*

Leading with Intent is a comprehensive nonprofit research project that offers a set of insightful practices for the board of directors based on their findings. What follows are five significant recommendations from *Leading with Intent: 2017 Index of Nonprofit Board Practices* (leadingwithintent.org). While there is a more updated version, the 2017 report recommendations fit here perfectly.

1. *Help your board cultivate a deeper understanding of your organization's work. Make it an ongoing priority to deepen your board's understanding of your organization's programs, service, products—what you do, why it matters, and how you know you have an impact.*

After having served as a chief executive staff member on a board for many years, I cannot underscore how important it is to help the trustees understand what the organization does and the justifications of why it matters.

2. *Create opportunities to build your board's comfort with and engagement in providing leadership outside of the boardroom. Think strategically and creatively about how to position board members for stronger leadership outside the boardroom through crucial social issues and broader community outreach.*

Apply strategic thinking to analyze the greater concepts about board engagement. Ask thoughtful, meaningful questions. This can encourage conscious board engagement. It also helps the board fulfill a significant obligation to your organization by bringing impactful outside issues to the board table.

3. *Explore and define your organization's values as it relates to diversity, inclusion, and equity. Start a conversation about what diversity means to your organization. What would a commitment to diversity, inclusion, and equity look like? What would it look like for your board, your organization, and your work in the community?*

Ideally, we want to get away from a more homogeneous board (race/culture, sexual identity, income, etc.) and reflect the communities we serve. This is an imperative and social justice action that should be nurtured across boards nationwide.

4. *Check in regularly on how well your board understands and is fulfilling its roles and responsibilities. Ensure that every board member starts his or her service with a firm understanding of his or her roles and responsibilities—what they are and what they aren't—and continually reinforce the importance of role understanding throughout every member's service.*

Boards need to understand their roles and responsibilities and distinguish them from what they aren't. This is a powerful statement. It trips up well-intentioned board members repeatedly. "Mission drift" is commonly referred to as chasing money and getting it from any source available as opposed to it being a good fit. However, this might be called "board drift," since board members can get confused about their roles. It can cause unattended rifts in the organization. Have the board chair clarify members' duties and obligations regularly.

5. *Invest in the board's culture. Work to cultivate a board culture of trust, respect, empathy, and mutual accountability within your board by creating opportunities for your members to engage with each other in a way that deepens their understanding of each other and their shared commitment to the organization's work.*

Some boards sponsor socials where no business is discussed and the purpose is just to get to know each other outside of the boardroom. There are many ways to accomplish this goal, but the idea is a nonjudgmental, non-work approach in becoming cohesive.

The just-mentioned remedies are critical solutions to board issues. Try them out as potential antidotes to the problems detailed in Chapter 17. These supports are so vital that they are worth mentioning frequently.

Out-of-the-box remedies for boards

"'A strong, vibrant board of directors is a clear indicator of a healthy organization,' according to the Maine Association of Nonprofits. 'Yet even the best organizations need a periodic checkup to ensure that they can not just survive but will really thrive in today's environment.' (Self-assessments for Nonprofit Boards)"

councilofnonprofits.org

Shared leadership

A concept for boards and staff working effectively together is shared leadership. An article by Richard Tollefson, founder and president of the Phoenix Philanthropy Group, talks about how shared leadership might work. "Shared leadership could start with a vision shared for the organization between the board of directors and the C.E.O. With that agreed upon, plans, strategies, and goals with the board and chief executive can follow." (See end of chapter for resources.)

Here are some key points

- Ideally, the board and staff can form constructive, equitable partnerships based on a healthy interdependency. A positive working relationship between the two entities (board and staff) is becoming imperative.
- Boards can develop the principles of a shared vision between themselves and staff, which is a vital organizational concept.
- Based on equality, we could begin to gradually redefine the roles of the CEO plus leadership staff and board members to reflect more equity.

- Our world is compelling boards to demonstrate their essential nature of support.
- Creating equal partnerships between the CEO and the board chair can augment social justice principles in a world that badly needs it.
- Equitable and effective leadership is a chance for companies to be a model for a new paradigm.
- With shared leadership, the board and key staff could discover jointly how to respect each other, have honest, open dialogue, suspend judgments, set mutual expectations, and celebrate their achievements.

The shared power standard addresses the power and control issues that often are established on a board. It's time that organizations lead the way in providing oversight that empowers board members and staff, while modeling the RESPECT principles to the communities served.

Rethink how to secure and train new board members

The Council of Nonprofits notes, "Many people serving on a nonprofit's board have never done so before, and others may have served on a nonprofit board that has different expectations for board members, so a basic discussion about the role of the board will help set consistent expectations." (See end of chapter for resources.)

The ways organizations come by (new) board members are fraught with problems. There is a sense of feeling lucky to find people willing to serve, whether appropriate or not. Yet, failing to find productive members who believe in the organization's values can have dire consequences for the business. Business does not have a reliable board recruiting and training process in place.

A quote from the insightful nonprofit business authority Joan Garry sums up board support: "Board service is a privilege. That working on behalf of your organization is a gift. That public service is the core to the betterment of society. The initial step to fix board recruitment would be to understand what board members are needed to do. In-depth conversation about what the CEO and current board chair think the organization needs in a board member at this time." (See end of chapter for resources.)

- Do the board candidates you're considering match the values of the organization and have the talents to implement these roles and responsibilities? Does the organization need a problem solver, a questioner of the status quo? Can they rise above power struggles? Use a discerning questioning process to help determine a candidate's suitability for the board.
- Cultivate and use screening tools that support the organization. You want trustees that can affect purposeful issues. Because of various circumstances, boards might be interested in people who exhibit some of the behaviors they like. However, these same persons might be incapable of performing the tasks the organization needs most. Do not settle. Timing can be a strategic tool.
- Do not let the vetting and securing of board members be random, which can lead to all sorts of problems. Figure out a way to let go of an incompetent member, even if other people aren't necessarily clamoring to become part of the board. An incompetent person can derail hard work.
- Additionally, boards may go through matrix mapping to ensure they acquire the skills, they are looking for. However, it can be an unproductive process because when the exercise is complete, an active board member leaves. Board terms don't mean much if someone wants to depart. Having been involved in board matrices in the past, I can say that they don't seem as practical as they are intended to be.

- The Nonprofit Resource Center cautions, "What's wrong is most board composition matrices focus attention on what people are, rather than what the organization needs board members to do."

Comprehensive and mandatory board orientations are necessary, no matter how many times a member has previously served. Most likely, that person hasn't served on your board before. And for new people, *their* orientation should be comprehensive and recurring. Note that there is a difference between orientation and training.

A board *orientation* might include:

- A meet-and-greet with the chief executive and/or board chair
- An explanation and demonstration of services and/or products
- A review of the expected roles and responsibilities that each board member plays
- Introductions to key staff
- A discussion of board and committee job descriptions and subsequent expectations
- A question-and-answer period
- Allot ample time. Do not rush this crucial orientation.

The above list gives you an idea of potential board orientation subjects to cover, but it is only a starting point. Generate your own list of essential subjects to cover. Board members can play a crucial role in how well a business functions. Make sure the person is right for the board.

Regular training for board members is a requirement if you desire that people will stay on task. Not clearly articulating what a potential board member is supposed to do can be dispiriting for both parties.

A board *training* could feature:

- The oversight and legal functions of a board
- How to execute a board's roles and responsibilities
- How to read financial reports
- How to evaluate the executive director
- How best to interact with staff and what are appropriate boundaries
- How to fundraise
- Succession planning for the board and how it translates to the executive director
- How to use strategic thinking for the utmost effectiveness
- An annual assessment of the board and what that means
- A review and discussion of the organization's bylaws

Grace Denny of Grand Valley State University sums it up: "Boards need to strategically recruit board members and provide orientation and ongoing training and education to members. Boards need to continuously evaluate their performance in achieving goals that they set for themselves and find ways to grow and improve." (See end of chapter for resources.)

Nonprofit boards require fundraising, or the field needs to change the requirements

A statistic cited earlier in this book noted that *only 29 percent of boards are active in fundraising.* As most executive directors can attest, you can bang your head against the proverbial wall trying to get help from boards with fundraising, to no avail. Even when there is a demonstrated need.

We can agree that boards provide fiscal oversight for business. So, they understand and know the financials reasonably well. Why then leave the onus on staff to provide all the fundraising that is needed? For clarity's sake, board members should either adhere to the condition of fundraising or have it removed from their duties.

Potential solutions with board fundraising in mind

- Regularly clarify the fundraising needs and expectations in conversations with the board. Whatever amounts the board decided on needs to materialize annually.
- The field could mandate comprehensive, readily available annual fundraising trainings for board members. The follow-up would be at (subsequent) board meetings to talk about practical techniques that members could try. For example, it could be a give-or-get policy, meaning one could write a personal check, obtain help from friends, or raise it themselves.
- The board could establish an ongoing adjunct volunteer committee that raises funds and reports back to the board.
- An alternative solution would be to retire the fundraising function from boards altogether.
- Currently, the expectation exists that boards fundraise. This element of board work needs to be understood and modified so that boards are on the same page as the requirements. Hopefully, soon, the nonprofit field will collectively agree on a board fundraising solution and implement it.

Apply the stages of board development to understand board duties and responsibilities

Ascertain what stage the board is currently at with a trustee discussion. Do expectations of board roles/activities need to be adjusted to reflect this developmental stage? Is it time to move to the next level or does the board function perfectly well at its current stage?

- Why would the board want to shift from one platform to another? Is it in better alignment with where the board is now? Does it make good strategic sense?
- If there is consensus for the board to go ahead with the move, then come up with a timeline and a plan for this significant change. Make sure all the key players are involved and know what to expect. Adjust board responsibilities as necessary. (See "The three stages in a board's life cycle" in Chapter 17.)

Practice using a social justice lens with the board

Employ social justice as a lens, a value, a mindset, and a mode of existing. Let's ensure we hear all voices, including those of board members, employees, and possible participants. It is due time that we began to look at board structure and infuse more social justice/equality into it.

Give board members a stipend or pay them to serve on your board

An article from the American Society of Association Executives addresses the question of board member compensation. While the article points out that board compensation is not illegal, there are things to consider. "On the plus side, compensation promotes economic diversity, allowing people to serve who might otherwise be unable to do so. Compensation also promotes professionalism rather than amateurism.

"Compensation can attract the most qualified individuals and values personal time and contributions. On the negative side, boards that pay members could discourage volunteering. Boards that pay people could also discourage charitable giving and boards that pay members could be considered the same as staff."

(See resources at the end of chapter.)

I have read articles with conflicting views on compensating board members. The important takeaway is that researchers have not found any link to nonprofit boards' competencies or diligence in undertaking their duties while paying board members to serve.

Create a national online certification program for boards and board chairs

A national online certification program could provide a more realistic understanding of a board, its chair, member roles, and its relationship to the organization. There is so much misunderstanding about what a board does and doesn't do. Some authorities call it role confusion.

One way to rectify it would be to create national standards for board roles, how a board operates, potential mandated roles and responsibilities training, and more equality for boards and staff.

I realize there are a host of issues involved with implementing a national online certification program for boards, including how it is handled and where the funding will come from. The idea is to give renewed hope to solving seemingly insurmountable obstacles by looking at numerous positive options.

Review and use the concept of Obligations of Boards

The responsibilities of care, loyalty, and obedience are powerful values to frame what boards are being asked to do. These duties highlight the trustees' legal and fiduciary duties. Board members are asked to put the organization's interests before their own personal interests, to take care in making decisions and to carry out its mission.

Following the principles of care, loyalty, and obedience can generate a more understanding and participatory board. Although the wording is formalized, don't let it deter you from benefiting from the actual meaning.

- Duty of Care: Intended to help boards exercise reasonable care when making strategic decisions about the assets of the organization.
- Duty of Loyalty: This is all about the mission of the enterprise and also asks members to disclose conflicts of interest.
- Duty of Obedience: Mandates the organization to enforce its bylaws and various regulations.

"I think if you care about someone and you got a little love in your heart, there ain't nothing you can't get through together."

Ted Lasso, on Apple TV +

Focus on "we" rather than "me"

As a board or staff member, you need to begin to focus more on considering the "we" than the "me." The emphasis should be on cooperation instead of separation. Why did you get on a board in the first place? Hopefully, it was to lend a hand, help advance the mission, and fortify the organization's critical path to success.

To achieve a "we" rather than a "me" means to put aside the "divide and conquer" mentality of the past. Agree to move to a different paradigm of running a business with the board and the staff. Ultimately, it's for the betterment of the community being served.

Accentuate compassion, understanding, and empathy

Establish (more) compassion, understanding, and empathy on the board. It is the bedrock or foundation of equality, empowerment, and justice. These are values that can activate the best of our human qualities. Board and staff need to work together to find solutions to problems.

Also, there is no one way of establishing a functioning board. Lead by example. Become an inspiration for others. We live in discouraging times.

Goals for staff and boards could come from a place of mutual understanding that collectively furthers the work in the community. Together we are facing tough issues and hard work. And most importantly, we cannot lose track of the bottom line: to positively impact the service (products, programs, etc.) we are providing for others.

Build communication skills

"We have become morally ill, because we have been accustomed to saying one thing and thinking another."

Vaclav Havel, Czech Dissident

Skilled communication is a skill that benefits everyone. Communications can be developed and practiced. The more you do it, the better a communicator you can become.

We could be worlds ahead by genuinely listening to each other's point of view and compromising at appropriate junctures. Active listening skills are vital since they remind us to receive the information coming our way.

> *"Most of what we do or don't do is based on our understanding of the messages that have been conveyed to us. In practical terms, misunderstandings can cost us time, money, credibility, and even relationships."*
>
> thinkedc.com

- Effective communication can become a valuable habit. This means becoming conscious of how you communicate at work, home, and in other places. It includes body language, how and what you say, listening, and writing skills. It can be an extra challenge if you throw in social media and all forms of electronic messaging.
- If the board is to be multicultural, which is critical, communication can get more involved. What means one thing to you may mean something entirely dissimilar to someone from another background. We need to understand that communication has its nuances, strengths, and pitfalls.

Fortunately, there are helpful communication programs available. Additionally, experienced facilitators can lead workshops about communication styles and the various limitations you could face.

Brainstorm the barriers to communication. Ask yourself the following questions:

- What communication pitfalls did you come up with, and how do these obstacles function in your communications with others?
- Have you gotten in touch with your own communication barriers? (Everyone has them.) Are you willing to work on them?
- How have communication difficulties been used against you? Have you had an incident where you have been verbally marginalized? How so?
- What are three things you can do this week to enhance your communications with others?
- What is the primary lens that you look through when communicating with a friend? Is it a different lens when you are talking with someone at work or with an adversary? How so?

Think about and answer these questions:

- Which items on your list of barriers are you guilty of or have had done to you?
- Why do you think this awkward communication occurred?
- Did this exercise help with an awareness of how you or others communicate?
- Healthy communication is a skill set. How will you work on your communication?

Communication barriers

- Not listening or poor listening skills
- Language differences

- Cultural differences
- Gender differences
- Status differences
- Using profanities in difficult conversations
- Differences in viewpoint and perceptions
- Prejudices
- Physical disabilities (hearing or speech problems)
- Emotional barriers and interactions
- Use of jargon
- Lack of interest or boredom
- Distractions
- Too much information
- Bad timing
- Unrealistic expectations

Add to this list; it's almost endless.

We communicate daily in small and also in very substantial ways. You may have noticed that it isn't easy to be an effective communicator. However, with practice and conscious awareness, we can get more proficient at it. Being a competent communicator is an attainable gift. Yet, we need to put effort into avoiding common barriers. Honing your communication know-how is a surefire way to enhance relationships.

Each of the components I've mentioned in this section might be classified as a unique resolution that can be debated or dismissed entirely as not having any possibility. If it starts a dialogue, positive or negative, then it has served a noble purpose. Numerous people in board and staff leadership positions think boards work great as they are. I say bravo.

However, I have experienced another, darker side of boards, one where it appears they are neither serving the organization nor the community they are helping. When they say power can corrupt, was it boards they were speaking about?

Power can be a great responsibility, and with it can come liberating freedoms. As board members, if we apply accountable solutions to the agency's issues, in the best possible way, we are truly exercising our duties. Then we can look forward to a future of positive change for all involved.

For-profit board ideas to put into practice

- Consider a thorough vetting process for each candidate who applies to be on your board.
- Engage trustees in annual or semi-annual role training. It is mandatory they understand their duties and execute them.
- Establish a board environment that encourages full participation.

Nonprofit board opportunities

- Pick a few board remedies (in this chapter) that board and staff could benefit from and implement them.
- Allow board members to derive meaning, inspiration, and satisfaction from their work on the board.
- Judiciously build a forward-looking board that can support your efforts in addressing the issues and getting the organization to a positive future.

Source: Adapted from McKinsey and Company, "The Board Perspective: A Collection of McKinsey Insights Focusing on Boards of Directors," mckinsey.com.

More board of director's research

- "Role Confusion on Nonprofit Boards: Promoting Board Engagement," Grace Denny, SPNHA Review, 2016, https://scholarworks.gvsu.edu/spnhareview/vol11/iss1/4/
- "Self-Assessments for Nonprofit Boards," National Council of Nonprofits, https://www.councilofnonprofits.org/tools-resources/self-assessments-nonprofit-boards
- "Ineffective Board Members in a Nonprofit Organization," BoardManagement.com, https://boardmanagement.com/blog/ineffective-board-members-in-a-nonprofit-organization/
- "How to Select First-Rate Board Members," Joan Garry, Joan Garry Consulting, https://blog.joangarry.com/interview-questions-non-profit-board-members/
- "Should Board Members of Nonprofit Organizations Be Compensated?" https://tinyurl.com/mwm66vym

Shared leadership

- "Shared Leadership: Today's Governance Board and Nonprofit CEOs Work Together," Richard Tollefson, The Giving Institute, August 1, 2014, https://tinyurl.com/24ez76du
- "Doing More with More: Putting Shared Leadership into Practice," Michael Allison, Susan Misra, and Elissa Perry, *Nonprofit Quarterly*, June 25, 2018, https://nonprofitquarterly.org/doing-more-with-more-putting-shared-leadership-into-practice/
- "Board Staff Partnership: How to Share Leadership & Get Results," BoardSource seminar offered through https://www.emilydavisconsulting.com/events/7258/. Note: This is an expensive seminar offered by a consultant through BoardSource, but it does give helpful highlights on what to expect

Teamwork

- "Why Nonprofit Teamwork Fails," Suzanne Smith, Social Impact Architects, July21, 2021, https://socialimpactarchitects.com/nonprofit-teamwork/
- "Build Teamwork into Your Company Culture," Susan M. Heathfield, The Balance, November 29, 2019, https://tinyurl.com/5eds8wv4

Books for boards of directors

- *Governance as Leadership: Reframing the Work of Nonprofit Boards*, Richard P. Chait, William P. Ryan, and Barbara E. Taylor. Wiley (2004)
- *Behind Boardroom Doors: Lessons of a Corporate Director,* Betsy Atkins. Miniver Press (2013).
- *Joan Garry's Guide to Nonprofit Leadership: Because Nonprofits Are Messy*, Joan Garry. Wiley (2017).
- *Corporate Board of Directors: Structure and Efficiency,* Ismail Lahlou. Palgrave Macmillan (2020).
- *Guidelines for Improving the Effectiveness of Boards of Directors of Nonprofit Organizations*, Vic Murray and Yvonne Harrison. Open SUNY Textbooks: Milne Library (2014).
- *Overcoming the Five Dysfunctions of a Team, A Field Guide for Leaders, Managers and Facilitators*, Patrick Lencioni. Jossey-Bass (2005).
- *The Handbook of Governance: A Comprehensive Guide for Public, Private and Not for Profit Board Members*, Richard Leblanc. Wiley (2016).

Chapter 19:
STAND FOR JUSTNESS
Social Justice

"Never doubt that a small group of thoughtful, committed citizens can change the world; indeed, it's the only thing that has."

Margaret Mead

Social Justice: *The objective of creating a fair and equal society in which each individual matters, their rights are recognized and protected, and decisions are made in a way that is fair and honest.*

oxfordreference.com

Social Movement: *A group of diffusely organized people or organizations striving toward a common goal relating to society or social change, or the organized activities of such a group.*

Dictionary.com

Social justice

This chapter is all about social justice. It is a vital concept for our world today. Social justice is about creating, supporting, and empowering community. It is impossible to achieve social justice in a vacuum. It is accomplished with others joining forces to inspire positive change. We cannot fix these problems alone.

The values in RESPECT (the S stands for social justice) come into play since there are principles involved in social justice. Empowerment, compassion, trust, resiliency, emotional intelligence, tenacity, and others. It is an attempt to right social wrongs.

It is a bit easier to understand how values play into social justice, but what about the bottom line of corporate profits? Some large, name-brand, for-profit corporations are excelling at applying values and putting their money where their mouths are. They accomplish this by helping causes such as the protection of endangered species, children with disabilities, or protecting the environment (to name a few). These same companies promote their achievement by advertising and subsequently giving generous donations to charitable endeavors.

Buyers support companies that they feel are doing good in the world. That way, some for-profit companies are living their values and adding to their profits. These successful companies are strong role models for others in business on how to live your values and make money.

It is time for a paradigm shift in how we think about social justice, and its benefits to humanity. It affects *all of us* in one way or another. By adding values and helping others, we can uplift ourselves to a higher octave of functioning and make money in the process.

Social justice can empower you, others, nonprofits, and for-profit businesses. It is a fix for all kinds of social ills. This chapter is more than just theory. It urges business to be regularly applying ideals to make the world a better place for *everyone.* Social justice principles can be considered stand-alones and apply to all topics in this book.

Social justice is intended to level the playing field. It ideally gives each person the opportunity to achieve. It can embrace equality in the most vital of ways.

And most of all, social justice speaks to the dignity of human beings. It implies people are getting their basic needs met. Social justice means everyone existing has the right to equity, regardless of race, gender, class, abilities, sexual orientation, or anything else. Politically, social justice refers to America's democracy and its social movements. We are aware there are conflicts related to specific social justice issues.

> *"I urge you to answer the highest calling of your heart and stand up for what you truly believe."*
>
> John Lewis. American statesman, and civil right activist

SOCIAL JUSTICE

Workers' rights
Disabilities
LGBT+
People of color rights
Housing equality
Women's rights
Environmental justice
. . . and much more

Social justice movements are carried out by groups of people who come together to advocate for fairness and bring attention to inequality and injustice. Think of social equity and justice as an intersecting web of awareness, education, and action. Social justice is the goal of a movement: for peace, economic and racial justice, and basic human respect and dignity, among many other qualities.

Plato and Aristotle both used the terminology and concept of social justice. This knowledge of fairness and equality has been around for an exceptionally long time. Social movements cover a vastness in their reach, as seen by the suffragettes working for women's right to vote or the nonviolent approach Martin Luther King advanced in the civil rights movement.

Social justice movements frequently originate from the "grassroots." This refers to a regular person from a local level who starts a political or economic campaign. People are motivated to take action and create systemic social change. *Social justice is the goal of social movements.* The objective of social movements is to gain equality for a particular group or population.

Social justice is usually the desired result of and reason for social movements. We are speaking to issues of inequity and inequality that have hurt millions of Americans for many centuries. Social justice can pertain to something specific, like raising the minimum wage, or more general, like workers' rights.

Since the 1960s, we have seemingly made gains in treating each other better. In the same breath, we still have so far to go. Social justice is a set of complex issues dealing with many aspects of society (with no easy fixes). A witness to this is the length of time these movements have been in existence. Many nonprofit organizations have a social justice orientation.

SOCIAL JUSTICE

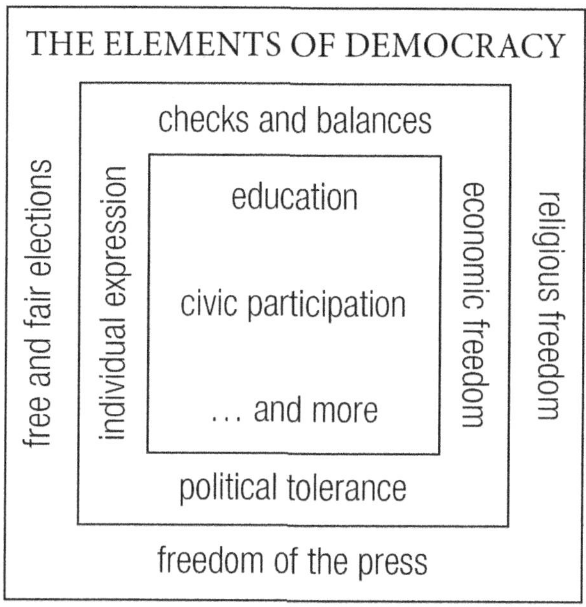

Democracy and social justice

Social justice holds that all people are entitled to the same fundamental rights and freedoms, promised to them by the documents of democracy. They both connect with issues of equity and equality. The United States of America is a democracy. The word "democracy" means "rule by the people." Ideally, this is social justice in action.

The principal purposes for which the People establish a democratic government are the protection and promotion of their rights, interests, and welfare."

The Concepts and Fundamental Principles of Democracy, civiced.org.

A democracy with a constitution tells its citizens that they have certain fundamental rights. These include freedom of religion/ conscience, economic freedom, political tolerance, freedom of the press, individual expression, transparency, free and fair elections, and more.

Democracy creates a foundational structure. This design shows social justice (and what it stands for) as part of its fundamental beliefs. Democracy embraces the many given freedoms as inalienable rights. Nonprofits and movements aid us by ensuring our liberties are intact. These human rights are needed to establish the equality and equity this country stands for.

Many organizations that serve people in some way support and empower citizens to know their rights and give voice to air issues. Yet it's humans who interpret the law. Even though we live in a democracy, many injustices persist.

"Prejudice is a great time-saver. You can form opinions without having to get the facts."

E.B. White

We know social justice attempts to right inequities. Yet, there are many unjust practices, violations, and problems related to human rights. This exercise will demonstrate the inequities and what harm they cause.

Instructions for social justice exercise

- Use three words from the list on the opposite page to describe each grouping mentioned: the words to user are personal, institutional, intentional, unintentional, prejudice, scapegoating, inequality, bias, illegal, unethical, unfair, discriminatory, and social grievances. Pick three.

- Match what you think best describe the words that begin with Poverty, etc. Try to use just three words (Personal, Institutional, etc.).
- Taking a whole sheet of paper, leave enough room so that each significant category (like racism) can have three words after it.

Poverty	Economic disparity
Race, ethnicity	Health care concerns
Native Americans	Religious or spirituality issues
Sexual orientation	Educational matters
Gender	Food insecurity
Black Lives Matter	Unemployment
COVID-19	Immigration
Special needs and mental health	Militarism
Women's issues, equal pay for equal work	Cultural diversity
Workers' rights, a living wage, unions, etc.	Homelessness
Ageism	Housing challenges
Environmental/ecological issues	Criminal justice, incarnation stats

Personal, Institutional, Intentional, Unintentional, Prejudice, Scapegoating, Inequality, Bias, Illegal, Unethical, Unfair, Discriminatory, and Social Grievances.

Please add to this list to include the social injustices you are most concerned with.

Process social justice exercise

- What words did you end up using the most, and why?
- Did you learn anything about yourself? Your business?
- Was it challenging to do this exercise? Why?

Money and power are connected

"An estimated 40 percent of the total U.S. population (140 million) are either poor or low-income."

ips.org

"Money is a medium of exchange; it allows people to obtain what they need to live."

Investopedia

Money is a system of trade. It's how people secure goods and services. Yet money is perhaps the greatest social justice issue we grapple with. Most global problems fall into the general category of inequality of funds. Money can seem to be at the heart of the problems with homelessness, racism, militarism, education, and so on.

Money produces anxiety for most people on our planet. Money is a strange phenomenon. It is despised, revered, hoarded; it's a panacea, there is entitlement, unequal distribution, and it produces fear.

Most of all, there's a power associated with it. It feels like someone else has the power, and others become "less than." Wars over money abound, Wall Street tries to control it, and women in the United States are *paid eighty-two cents for every dollar paid to men,* according to nationalpartnership.org.

"Commercialization and inequality reinforce the power of money as a barrier to positive social change."

Michael Edwards, opendemocracy.net

Power and money are linked. You don't have to look any further than America's top politicians in the White House and the Senate to see how wealth and power are related. Intentionally or not, we have long accepted an attitude that someone rich has more privilege, better possessions, appears happier, and often holds power.

So many social justice issues center around how money and power seem to be against the "regular" folk in society. *"Power over"* is an unhealthy manifestation of this. It demonstrates the countless social justice issues locally and worldwide. It can happen anywhere.

"Worker hourly compensation has flat-lined since the mid-1970s, increasing just 24 percent from 1979 to 2018, while worker productivity has increased 134 percent over the same time period."

Economic Policy Institute, Policy Agenda, epi.org

Money is just a currency exchange. I buy a jacket; I give money or credit in return for this merchandise. It is humans who put their spin on it. In today's world, money has become a measure of our value, status, position, power, and authority.

It is a way for others to dominate the less fortunate. Within all the major issues we are facing in the world, especially in the US, wealth and power are front and center. We need money to live on, yet it is not evenly distributed.

"Gaps in earnings between America's most affluent and the rest of the country continue to grow year after year."

inequality.org

Think About Money

- How we feel about finances usually comes from our family of origin. Does it work the same way organizationally? Bring awareness and make a list of any institutional beliefs you can think of regarding financial resources.
- Do you have enough money personally and to run your business?
- Do you blame the establishment or persons for not having enough of what you want or need?

- Does it feel okay to have an adequate or more than enough income?
- Can you talk about money with others? Why or why not?
- In the social justice arena, what are the responsibilities of having money, and how are they adhered to?
- Is money a positive force for organizational or social justice transformation?

Social justice: from the voice of a child

My daughter, Naomi, came home from elementary school one afternoon. She was eight at the time. Naomi was upset. I asked what was wrong. She said that on the playground during recess, her friend Ruby was picked on and made fun of by other children. I knew from play dates that Ruby was African American. My heart sank as Naomi cried and told me the story. Two things were apparent:

1. Ruby was the victim of bullying.
2. Ruby became the target because she was "different." Ruby was African American with brown skin amongst a sea of white children.

Naomi asked me why the kids were so mean to Ruby. Not quite knowing what to say to a young child about race, I paused and then replied, "It is the color of her skin." My daughter looked incredulous, and said, "No, Mommy, what's the real reason?" I said, "That's the real reason." Naomi said, "But, Mommy, that doesn't make sense."

Racism and the other "isms" make no sense. They are simply not believable as actions or concepts. They represent differences that people assign to all kinds of issues because they feel uncomfortable. The perpetrator of these misconceptions also gets to feel better than the other person. Yet, I was taught that in religion, we were all equal regardless of circumstance.

Think about social justice

- Does the organization you are a part of (or like) have a social justice cause? What does it do, and why is it important?
- What is an obstacle that the business must overcome to help further a social justice cause?
- Is there a social justice issue around money at the enterprise where you are employed?
- What kinds of results would the business want to see from its social justice actions (if it has any)?

I know the organization I ran for twenty five years endeavored to have a positive social justice impact on participants. Social impact in this context means that services were empowering enough to encourage participants to make their voices heard and ask meaningful questions no matter what the concern was. Also, it gave individuals problem-solving opportunities with staff.

Business needs to be more caring. We live in a world that doesn't necessarily act on values of kindness and consideration. I understand that to level the playing field, it will take a substantive paradigm shift.

Companies working in a social justice capacity can model light for a dark world that lacks hope. Movements add tremendously to the social justice capacity of an organization to shift the needle on global injustices.

It's essential to continue with relatively small steps to tackle these key problems.

These steps can take us in the right direction. Concerted, ongoing action is required to solve the current obstructions related to social inequalities in the world.

Here are two examples of social justice movements

People with disabilities

"People with disabilities are among the most marginalized groups in history."

Ten facts on disability, World Health Organization, who.int

"The disability rights movement has been working to break institutional, physical and societal barriers that prevent people with disabilities living their lives like other citizens."

A Brief History of Disability Rights and the Americans with Disabilities Act (ADA), Phil Pangrazio, ability360.org

Congress passed the far-reaching Americans with Disabilities Act (ADA) and said in part, *Disabilities are a natural part of the human experience.* July 26, 2020, marked the thirtieth anniversary of the ADA. The disability rights movement, like many social justice movements, has shed light on a long and shameful history of discrimination. In 1846, an "idiot" law stated,

"No white person shall intermarry with a negro, and no insane person or idiot shall be capable of contracting marriage."

A Brief History of Disability Rights and the Americans with Disabilities Act (ADA) by Joe Ability, *LivAbility Magazine*, ability360.org

People with disabilities, to this day, do not get equal treatment as citizens in the US. Access remains a prominent civil and political rights issue facing this group. The broad intention has been to secure equity and opportunities in all areas for people with disabilities.

> *"Americans with disabilities are a group of approximately 40.7 million people that today lead independent, self-affirming lives and who define themselves according to their personhood—their ideas, beliefs, hopes and dreams—above and beyond their disability."*
>
> A Brief History of the Disability Rights Movement, wwwadl.org

Disability rights advocates have reshaped the very landscape of our country. Their mobilization and consistent defense of disability rights is the reason changes have come about.

These supportive modifications include but are not limited to accessibility on all fronts, including reasonable accommodations at the workplace and other environments, universal design on products, accessible transportation, state and local governments working in tandem with disability advocates, and much more.

In short, the changes made to America because of disability rights consist of access, more equality, and the possibility for a brighter future. This also implies a better understanding of what it means to be a disabled person. Remember, *disability does not equate to an inability to achieve, (*sae.edu.au.)

Environmental injustice

Definition of environmental justice: All people and communities have the right to equal environmental protection under the law, and the right to live, work, and play in communities that are safe, healthy, and free of life-threatening conditions. E J definitions (E=environmental J= justice), columbia.edu.

Today, there are serious environmental challenges. There are too many to cite. However, some worth noting include: global warming, unprecedented levels of all types of pollution, household and industrial waste disposal, public health issues, and powerful special interest groups that defeat laws meant to safeguard us. The laundry list of offenders undermining our basic protections is much greater than what's in the daily news.

Despite what was just mentioned, there is good news. A very active environmental movement that helps address these issues exists. Fortunately, it didn't just start. Many early environmental justice leaders came out of the civil rights movement. They brought the same tools that proved successful in the fight for civil rights.

These organizing strategies (useful in today's social justice struggles) embraced peaceful demonstrations, campaigns, rallies, fostering alliances, nonviolence, empowerment through education, and litigation.

Within this movement there are four areas of focus that Robert Doyle Bullard, known as the father of environmental justice, has identified. They include:

1. *Obstructions regarding environmental issues*
2. *Environmental health risk discrepancies*
3. *Economic inequalities*
4. *Racial disparities*

Nothing in recent times describes Bullard's four points more effectively than the Flint, Michigan, water crisis. It began in 2014 when the City of Flint made a cost-saving decision to switch the city's water source from Detroit to the Flint Fiver. This move resulted in sickeningly contaminated water.

It was reported that the water was foul smelling, discolored, and off tasting. It created hair loss, skin rashes, and elevated blood pressure among other health issues. The problems from this "dirty" water continued. At least twelve people died and eighty became sick of Legionnaires' disease.

There was inadequate testing and treatment of water and underqualified staff that ran the program. This equaled gross mismanagement of Flint's drinking water. Flint serves as a reminder that safe, drinkable water is not a guarantee.

It's important to note that Flint is over 50 percent African American, and almost half of Flint's population is living in poverty. Flint has one of the highest poverty rates among US cities (stats from the US Census Bureau).

A lawsuit of 600 million dollars has been allocated for the victims of the Flint, Michigan, water disaster. It is the largest settlement ever in that state. In addition, the governor at the time, Rick Snyder, has been charged with two counts of willful neglect.

Eight other bureaucrats were charged with thirty-four felony counts and seven misdemeanors for their role in the crisis. While some would say these officials got their "just desserts," it's hard to imagine the life of a child threatened because of willful "neglect" making it such that any dollar amount would be worth it.

Environmental justice has a vitally important objective in today's world: save the planet from abject misuse. There are potential solutions to these environmental issues, although time is of the essence. Yet, with resolve, outcomes in mind, and persistence, "we shall overcome."

We can borrow strategies from successful movements, use research and studies to prove the points on environmental injustice, insist on fair and transparent decision-making, and involve as many stakeholders as possible. Activism matters and is vital when we speak of these inequities.

"We want to support a shift from consumption to sharing, from competition to collaboration. Only by increasing our collective responsibility for each other, can we build a green and peaceful future."

A portion of the Greenpeace vision statement, Greenpeace International, greenpeace.org

People power! Grassroots leadership in the social justice movement

"If you see something, say somethin."

Allen Kay

There is a demand for leaders to become the heroes and heroines (not martyrs) for social justice. The cry is being heard. Help strengthen the principles of democracy. Dismantle the old structures on injustice, inequality, dishonesty, and money. Make room for balance to emerge. Rebuild our world, so it becomes a more equitable space for everyone.

We as members of humanity are in enormous flux, as witnessed by the recent coronavirus pandemic that has affected most of us on the planet. This virus has impacted the federal government, health care, travel, education, the economy, jobs, nonprofits, stores, restaurants, and much more.

If you're already a leader in a business but are thinking about leading a cause, do it. Humankind needs you, and we are ripe for necessary and constructive changes. Even if you're not a current leader, that doesn't mean you cannot become one.

If you're full of passion for a cause and know something corrupt can be different, perhaps it's time to step up into the role of a leader.

If it's behind the scenes, fine. It doesn't matter. What matters is your firm intention to make a change for the better in the world.

Knowing what it takes to be a leader can be pivotal in social justice success. There are leadership skills that transcend the mundane and are worthy of replication.

"Great leadership begins with the person, not the position."

Leadership Skills: 8 Principles Every Leader Should know, foucs3.com

Leadership qualities are much debated, with different experts offering lists of few or many characteristics that go into effectively playing a leadership role. However, what I do know is that leadership traits are different for each person. Some attributes, though, surpass boundaries. Ultimately, you need to feel dedicated and passionate about a social justice cause and want good to come from it.

Additionally, you can bring beneficial behaviors and a set of disciplines to leadership. Positive guidance is about listening, not necessarily agreeing, but genuinely listening. Then it's about knowing how to follow and when to lead and driving a fruitful change. It is also vital to know what you want to accomplish.

Use your imagination for a second. Pretend that a nonprofit leader has asked you to head up a volunteer social justice activity. Regrettably, they do not have the bandwidth to make it happen with staff alone. This movement or other action could benefit hundreds if not thousands of people. You don't consider yourself a leader but are interested. What qualities would you need to be successful?

Leadership qualities

An exercise in leadership

Make a list of ideal leadership qualities you think you would need to lead people through a social justice action. Now compare it with the list compiled below. What's not on the list that is necessary? Add what is meaningful to you and subtract what isn't.

Potential leadership qualities

- Lead by example
- Focus on and drive change
- Promote diversity
- Inspire and/or add your charisma to an issue
- Have a passion for the values you are fighting for
- Be inclusive and flexible enough to share power with others
- Have courage, patience, tenacity, empathy, purpose, and vision
- Have emotional intelligence and dexterity
- Have a group of workers willing to roll up their sleeves
- Know your goals and what you are trying to accomplish

Please add your favorite leadership qualities to the list if you don't see them above.

Can you be a social justice leader? Can you lead a cause you are passionate about and create real change? You are stronger than you think and have the qualities needed to pull this off. Know that you do not need all the traits listed. Select the ones you already have or would like to develop and follow through.

Another consideration is that you don't have to lead alone. A second person could complement your skills and abilities and co-chair the movement, action, or event. You can divvy up your duties based on your strengths and move the needle on your cause.

Think about these social justice questions

- Name one social justice issue or movement you are involved in or want to be. Could you lead it? Why or why not?
- Why is this particular social justice value (mentioned above) important to you?
- Can you join forces with an organization that has a similar cause and blend your work with what they do?
- Have you or someone you know ever been excluded or singled out from something related to your quality of life that upset you—that seemed unfair? Describe the situation. Did you do anything to change it?
- Do you believe we have made progress over the last ten years in the entire social justice movement or just in sectors?
- What steps could a business take to incorporate more social justice perspectives and initiatives into the workplace (excluding affirmative action sort of responsibilities)?

Social justice is a movement, an ideal, and a philosophy that people embrace. It's a whole way of seeing and living life differently. It's taking action regarding injustices that affect you and your family and/or people in your community. Your involvement and commitment to these issues matters.

It's great if you want to be involved in specific causes, but it can be hard to know where to turn. Universities act as a clearinghouse of information, as do large nonprofits like the Southern Poverty Law Center, the Transgender Law Center, the National Organization for Women, and the Task Force for Global Health.

Fortunately, or not, these organizations have niches and specialize in a particular area of social justice. The field of social justice is compartmentalized into areas that are being addressed and worked on. It would be great, however, if social justice had a one-stop shop or a type of clearinghouse for all types of information.

Social injustice: The perfect setup

In Chapter 17 on boards, I included a cautionary board tale about my own experience. I described how the board was unhappy with my work performance. They wanted me gone. This is the account of how they got their wish.

There were several staff who I thought well of and knew of the board's ongoing dissatisfaction regarding my management style. Distressingly enough, they decided to lead the charge and help the board get rid of me. They peppered the trustees with stories of my alleged inappropriate interactions with them and others.

The gathering of documentation and narrative regarding my assumed harmful actions went on secretly for about three months by these same personnel. To make matter worse, one of these people wanted my job. This person who was eyeing my role also considered himself to be best buddies with the board chair.

Additionally, I was misled about why the investigator was coming in. I was informed by the employee who sought my position that the examiner would be questioning the firings of some challenging staff that I let go. So, I was prepared to answer questions about these past employees.

Few people in the organization knew what was transpiring (including me). I regard myself as a perceptive person. However, I was totally blindsided by the elevated levels of duplicity.

Several weeks before meeting with the investigator, I received an email from the board. The gist of it was this:

You will have an opportunity to share your concerns about this probe, the board, the process, etc. with the investigator.... it is vital to uphold the spirit of fairness....

We believe this process is grounded and in our shared values of social and restorative justice.

The board gave me their assurance they would uphold social and restorative justice, and fairness. These are values that I believed in and founded the organization on. Yet, I was never given a chance to defend myself. I was invisible and yet central to the investigation. It seemed a direct contradiction with what the board had said about *upholding the spirit of fairness.*

It came to a head in early February 2019. The trustees hired an attorney who specialized in HR investigations to review complaints against me. In a ninety-minute meeting with just the two of us, the solicitor started off by saying that he decided people's fates based on the evidence he received.

I knew in that moment; I had already been found guilty. I was simultaneously disoriented and utterly crushed. It was a painful review of my presumed wrongdoings, yet I was ill equipped to defend myself.

I was undone by the betrayals and ushered almost immediately out the door after my meeting with the lawyer, not to return. However, the devastating anguish that I experienced supported me in carrying out a meaningful dive into old, undermining patterns of my behavior.

It has been an exceptionally challenging, yet surprisingly heartening, journey. I intuitively applied the concepts of R.E.S.P.E.C.T. to my recovery. It helped me regain my self-esteem and mend the psychological breach of the betrayals that occurred. These days, I am breathing great sighs of relief to be complete with this part of my life.

I am grateful that I had the opportunity to grow, change, learn, and connect with this lovely participant-driven community for twenty-five years. I am honored to have served the remarkable families and establish notable bonds with special people in the nonprofit field.

Hopefully, what happened at the business I founded is not enough to diminish the fundamental essence of an organization that embeds itself in social justice, resiliency, empowerment, and the rest of the values mentioned in these chapters.

Social justice comes about because of a social movement or a cause. Our democracy through our Constitution promises us life, liberty, and the pursuit of happiness. However, these values are stalled, as seen in daily examples of social injustice. We must continue social justice movements to address the issues of fairness and equality.

Social justice can give us the leg up to form a new world that places empowerment and other values first. It might be a considerable paradigm shift, but it is a necessary one. Each individual needs to have the same freedoms and rights as the next person. Since we are all in this together, let's realize that and begin to work together to solve all these problems we ourselves have created. Let's lead the way with the value of justness.

For-profit ideas on social justice to put into practice

- For-profit business is about making money. Social justice and for-profits are odd bedfellows. Yet, money can be put to suitable use in countless causes. Invest in social justice.
- Social justice and business have commonalities that include empowerment through acquiring knowledge and forming connections.
- Remember to promote qualified women, people of color, and others that are historically discriminated against.

Nonprofit social justice opportunities

- Social justice necessitates that the workplace be equitable in its treatment of employees. List out how you think this is already happening or can be achieved.
- Be willing to really hear staff and learn what they believe to be their fundamental rights related to equality and fairness in the workplace.
- Nonprofits are poised to provide leadership in many of the social movements of today. Identify people who are passionate and can lead a cause. Get them trained now.

More research on social justice

- "The Concepts and Fundamental Principles of Democracy," Center for Civic Education, https://www.civiced.org/pdfs/books/ElementsOfDemocracy/Elements_Subsection3.pdf
- "Money: In Terms of Social Change, It's Both Beauty and the Beast," Michael Edwards, Open Democracy, February 18, 2014, https://www.opendemocracy.net/en/transformation/money-in-terms-of-social-change-its-both-beauty-and-beast/
- "Poor People's Moral Budget: Everybody Has the Right to Live," Institute for Policy Studies, 2019, https://ips-dc.org/report-moral-budget-2/
- "Policy Agenda," Economic Policy Institute, December 2018, https://www.epi.org/policy/
- Compensation Research, US Bureau of Labor Statistics, https://www.bls.gov/crp/
- "A Brief History of Disability Rights and the Americans with Disabilities Act (ADA)," Phil Pangrazio and Joe Ability, LivAbility Magazine, July 14, 2015, https://ability360.org/livability/advocacy-livability/history-disability-rights-ada/

- "10 Facts on Disability," World Health Organization, https://www.who.int/news-room/facts-in-pictures/detail/disabilities
- Blog posts by Dr. Adam Foley, Office of Equity and Inclusion, University of Delaware, https://sites.udel.edu/oei/category/adam-foley/
- Social Problems: Continuity and Change, Open Textbook, University of Minnesota Library, 2016, https://open.umn.edu/opentextbooks/textbooks/141
- "Environmental Justice," Columbia University, https://sustainable.columbia.edu/content/environmental-justice#:~:text=What%20is%20Environmental%20Justice%3F,redress%20historical%20and%20cumulative%20harms
- "8 Qualities of Strong Leadership and How to Become a Stronger Leader," Indeed Editorial Team, May 24, 2021, https://www.indeed.com/career-advice/career-development/strong-leadership
- "10 Reasons Why Social Justice is Important," Human Rights Careers, https://www.humanrightscareers.com/issues/10-reasons-why-social-justice-is-important/
- "What Is Social Justice?" Pachamama Alliance, https://www.pachamama.org/social-justice/what-is-social-justice
- "What Is Social Justice?" Dorothy's Place, https://www.dorothysplace.org/social-justice/
- "Aggression and Violence," GoodTherapy.com, https://www.goodtherapy.org/learn-about-therapy/issues/aggression-violence

Books

- *Readings for Diversity and Social Justice, 4th edition*, Maurianne Adams et al., eds. Routledge (2018).
- *Advocacy Practice for Social Justice, 4th edition*, Richard Hofer. Oxford University Press (2019).
- *Transforming Communities: How People Like You Are Healing Their Neighborhoods*, Sandhya Rani Jha. Chalice Press (2017).

Chapter 20:
BOUNCE BACK
Resiliency

"You may encounter many defeats, but you must not be defeated. Please remember that your difficulties do not define you. They simply strengthen your ability to overcome."

Maya Angelou

Resiliency: *An ability to recover from or adjust easily to misfortune or change*

Merriam-Webster

Resiliency means knowing how to cope despite setbacks, barriers, or limited resources. It's what gives us the psychological strength to manage stress and hardship. Resiliency has come to signify mechanisms for protection against harmful events. It has become a common buzzword for recovery of many kinds.

This chapter speaks to the qualities of resiliency and how to nurture it. Resiliency helps to maintain equilibrium. The good news is that it is never too late to develop our innate resiliency.

Any enterprise worth their salt develops organizational and employee resiliency. If people at the company are taught how to cope with a difficult situation professionally, it can ultimately aid the business in persevering while steadying the ship. It's a graceful way out of danger and can help increase the company's profits by learning what to do, how to do it, and how to bounce back after adversity.

I am describing resiliency as a value that adds substantial benefits to any company. It allows us to face the threats that are inherent in business, it energizes us to embrace new opportunities, and it helps us learn how to handle collective stress.

Resiliency gives us the stamina and courage to take measures against all the inequity, prejudices, biases, and injustices and come back to a sense of justice.

Resiliency gives us flexibility and strength that allows us to bounce back after significant challenges. It helps us to mend, especially psychologically, from the many indignities we experience in a lifetime. Writing in The *New York Times*, Eilene Zimmerman noted, "The tools common to resilient people are optimism (that is also realistic), a moral compass, religious or spiritual beliefs, cognitive and emotional flexibility, and social connectedness." (See resources at the end of the chapter.)

Research proves resiliency works

I first learned of resiliency in the late 1980s, from Bonnie Bernard, MSW. She disseminated this information (particularly) in the Bay Area of California. She had numerous speaking engagements, published multiple informative articles, and started a publication on resiliency that ran for a number of years. Through these channels, Bernard helped show the field how to embed resiliency in youth development programs.

Most importantly, Bernard brought to light the long-range resiliency studies by sociologist Emmy Werner. Werner's noteworthy research gave hope to youth that had immeasurable challenges to overcome. These young people from high-risk environments not only survived, but 50 to 70 percent of them thrived. Werner and her team identified the social competencies that helped children beat the odds because of resiliency.

In Bernard's article, called "The Foundations of the Resiliency Framework," she wrote, "We are all born with innate resiliency. We possess the capacity to develop traits commonly found in resilient survivors. These traits are social competencies. These include problem-solving skills, autonomy, and adaptive distancing from negative messages and conditions and a sense of purpose and belief in a bright future. The significant point here is that resilience is not a genetic trait that only a few 'super kids' possess, but rather it is our inborn capacity for self-righting (Werner and Smith 1992) and for transformation and change (Lifton 1993)." (See resources at the end of the chapter.)

This quote illustrates the essential nature of resiliency. Anyone can access the ability to bounce back. It lives within us. Life is full of problems and unexpected twists and turns. It is noteworthy that in our human coping skills, we have the inherent psychological strength to overcome stress and hardship.

The *New Yorker* ran a thought-provoking article on resiliency called "How People Learn to Become Resilient." It cited respected researcher and educator George Bonanno, a clinical psychologist at Columbia University's Teachers College. He heads the Loss, Trauma, and Emotions Lab and has been studying resiliency for more than thirty years. His research has been to observe people and ask: *Do we conceptualize an event as traumatic or as an opportunity to learn and grow?*

Bonanno was quoted in the article (by Maria Konnikova, the *New Yorker*, February 11, 2016) as saying: "We can make ourselves vulnerable by how we think about things. Events are not agonizing until we feel them as agonizing. Resiliency is the ability to repair ourselves as opposed to just enduring the crisis and waiting for it to pass." (See resources at the end of the chapter.)

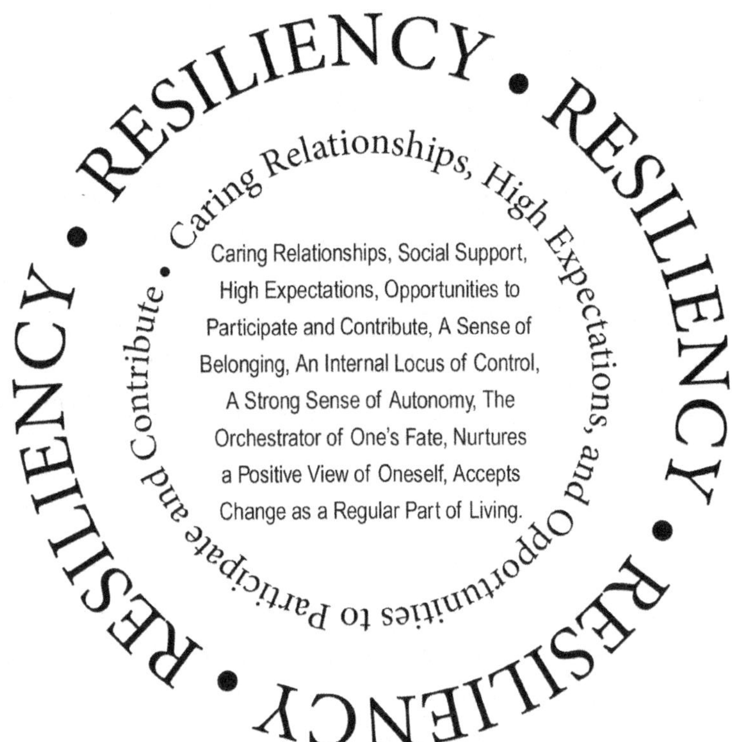

Bonanno's quote in The *New Yorker* article is motivating us to understand and practice resiliency. We are influenced, often unconsciously, by our attitudes, thinking, and beliefs, are mirrored back to us by our emotions. How we think or feel about a potentially difficult incidence will determine how it will impact us either positively or negatively.

A story about applying resiliency

As an illustration, let's use the birth of a baby. While many would consider it a positive, life-affirming event, some parents might not describe it that way.

There may be extenuating circumstances, such as unplanned single parenthood, not enough money, postpartum depression in the mom, inadequate or inappropriate housing, complicated relationships surrounding the new mom, disabilities in the infant, and so on

Resiliency means we expand our emotions, use the environment to our betterment, rely on religion or our version of spirituality and our support network to recuperate from a potentially hard situation.

The mom experiencing any of these complications can reduce issues by varying degrees through applying resiliency concepts. These approaches might include using our social networks or connectedness to others, how we think and feel regarding the situation (cognitive and emotional flexibility), and having the expectation that we will recover (optimism).

Resiliency doesn't mean that we don't suffer (unfortunately). It demonstrates that this place of disruption, of upheaval, doesn't need to be permanent. Resiliency proves that we can recover our sense of optimism and build new motivation, even if it takes time (which it often does). We can learn a lot about ourselves from our misfortunes.

Resiliency is a process that helps us go to a better, more empowered place in our lives. It has us shaking our heads and thinking, "If this didn't happen, I might not have met this person who changed my life for the better, or I never would have realized how much this person loved me or just how strong I am," or something to that effect.

> *"Resiliency is about getting through pain and disappointment without letting it crush your spirit."*
>
> psychologytoday.com

Think about resiliency

Reflect on a time you recovered from a challenging situation.

- What steps did you take that were most helpful for your healing?
- How challenging was this situation to overcome on a scale of 1–10 (10 connoting the highest challenge)?
- How long did it take you to improve your emotional and mental health?
- What was most instrumental in your recovery? Was it your faith or spirituality, your family, journaling, a circle of friends, or professional help? Or something else?
- Was it a gradual process, or did it seem to happen fairly quickly?
- Did anything good come from this problem(s)?
- Do you consider yourself a resilient person? Why or why not?

Change and loss are inevitable parts of humanity and living life. We know that resilience is an overall factor in the recovery of adversity. The best news is that we all possess resiliency. It is healthy human development.

Growing your coping abilities helps you to discover "personal gifts" from life's problems and challenges. It does not mean that becoming more resilient eliminates stress or erases life's difficulties. As you become more resilient, you spend less time worrying about the "could have, should have, would haves."

The three protective factors

"Protective Factors are individual or environmental characteristics, conditions, or behaviors that reduce the effects of stressful life events. These factors also increase an individual's ability to avoid risks or hazards and promote social and emotional competence to thrive in all aspects of life, now and in the future."

Adolescent and School Health, cdc.gov.
(See resources at the end of the chapter.)

1. Caring relationships
2. High expectations
3. Opportunities to participate and contribute

Protective factors are another way to think about resiliency. Consider protective factors as important pieces of resiliency. They are the skills that appear to alter or even reverse potentially negative outcomes. These are properties relating to our personality that actually seem to cushion threats.

Werner's research demonstrates these protective factors are essential for developing the ability to recover from difficulties. Caring relationships and high expectations are crucial to nurturing protective factors in childhood and adolescence.

Supportive qualities such as these often come from the same concerned adult. It could be someone in the family unit or outside the home, like a teacher or a coach. This person believes in the youth's potential and serves as their cushion in a challenging environment.

Also, in many cases, a helpful adult can steer the youth to meaningful opportunities to participate and contribute. In other words, to have a caring grown-up in the life of a "high-risk" child can mitigate the major challenges they face.

Protective factors have taken on a life of their own. They embed themselves in standards for various networks that advocate for a particular cause. For instance, a national movement to prevent child abuse has five protective factors that help to create an optimal environment for children. (See the infographic "How to Remember the 5 Protective Factors That Make Your Family Strong," at thefyi.org.)

Let's build up protective factors through adding strengths to one's innate resiliency. How can we accomplish this goal? One of the ways would be to apply the competencies described by Bonnie Bernard's resiliency.

Tier 1 consists of the essential protective factors and adds to it. Tiers 2 and 3 play supporting roles.

This trio of protective factors offers tips on how one might use and sustain resiliency. These are indispensable resources for an adult's development. Additionally, they can aide a child and adolescent's development (if it's age-appropriate).

Instructions: Look at the three tiers of Building Resiliency; Match the 1–3 tiers with the questions that best fit where you are at with your levels of resiliency.

Ask Yourself these questions about resiliency

- What personality characteristics do I currently have (as one heading)
- What do I want to focus more attention on and strengthen (as another heading)?
- What holds me back from creating a stronger sense of resiliency (third heading)?
- What is one action per week from the list below that I can think about and grow in myself?

BUILDING RESILIENCY		
1st Tier	**2nd Tier**	**3rd Tier**
Develops mutual, caring relationships	Makes realistic plans and sticks to them	Good-natured
Nurtures high expectations in self and others	Implements self-help skills	Feel the viewpoint or judgments one might have when "buttons get pushed" and then move on to problem solving
Builds social support: friends, family, whoever helps strengthen one in times of trouble	Is an effective communicator and a good listener	Free of distressing habits
Establishes opportunities to participate and contribute	Doesn't play the victim role	Has special interests and hobbies

1st Tier	2nd Tier	3rd Tier
Creates a sense of belonging to a community	Sees things through and perseveres (understands there is a light at the end of the tunnel)	Possesses emotional intelligence
Holds a positive view of oneself and one's abilities	Nurtures the skill to focus attention and control impulses	Walking one's talk
Embraces autonomy and independence	Works on a positive self-concept like self-esteem	The ability to improvise
Exercises a moral compass	Practices gratitude	Acceptance of the nature of reality
Uses an internal locus of control so that one believes that he, and not his circumstances, affects his achievements or challenges	Possesses a sense of humor	Makes time for self-care
Experiences mental and emotional flexibility		

Add to this list any strength-based tool that is important for you when overcoming hardship.

Richard Wiseman, a psychology professor at the University of Hertfordshire, was quoted as saying, "Changing a personality trait requires acting in ways that embody that quality, rather than simply thinking about it. The Act as If principle allows you to behave as if you are the person you want to be. Pretty soon, you might find that it is you." (See resources at the end of the chapter.)

Resiliency in action

An instance of organizational resiliency occurred at the family center in 2002. As previously mentioned, we bought the building that housed the center in 2000 and began renovation two years later. Around this time, California, along with the support of a well-known actor and activist, established a fund to support children up to age five and their families resulting from a state tobacco tax.

Officials wanted the tobacco tax to make tobacco products more expensive so that it would cut down on folks purchasing and using them. It included a precaution about second-hand smoke as well. It would give nonprofits (that qualified) the much-needed funds for serving children and their families.

A percentage of tobacco tax dollars went to local counties in California to finance early childhood development programs. There was an established precedent in the Bay Area for family centers that shared universal principles of how services/programs are offered to children five and under.

The city received this funding and created a municipal agency to award dollars to local nonprofits. The first grant application from them came out in the early 2000s. The organization I ran applied for it.

I was excited about it since it would nearly double the amount of money we were receiving for family and parent/child activities with toddlers. However, these planned services needed a larger inside area, and we hadn't even begun our renovation. I was nervous. What were we going to do if we got the money and the section of space for the expanded programs wasn't ready?

As it turned out, my worrying was unnecessary. This initial grant process was thrown out. One of the grant application readers worked at a nonprofit that had also requested a portion of this money. It was a conflict of interest. As agencies that applied for these funds, we fought the potential awards since it seemed inherently unfair.

I was disappointed that we had to reapply and wait until the following year. Yet it became one of those blessings in disguise. When the next proposal came out a year later, we requested support. Happily, we received all the funding we asked for and simultaneously completed our renovation. Phew! We began the increased services in our newly renovated space in July 2003. Families were pleased with our expanded services. We persevered and became more organizationally flexible.

Instruction on organizational resiliency exercise

Go through each statement and determine how resilient your business is by giving it a numerical rating of 1–5, with 5 being the highest. Then process this exercise using the rating approach below. One can also go through this exercise by having a department in mind of a large corporation.

What is organizational resiliency?

Organizational resiliency (the ability to bounce back) is strong at our organization and will see us through possible threats we face.

We thrive at, anticipate, and respond positively and productively to change.

We have engaged competent and effective leadership at the board and staff level.

Staff most often responds constructively and calmly to problematic events.

Employees feel energized by new opportunities.

The business readily adapts to new or unforeseen circumstances or events.

The agency bounces back from problematic situations to become stronger and better.

Our enterprise handles collective stress well.

At the organization, one lives by the philosophy that avoiding calculated risks becomes missed opportunities.

Think about this organizational resiliency exercise

If your overall score was 1 or 2, you should pay attention to the resiliency research and how strength and flexibility develop. How you overcome adversity is key to understanding coping mechanisms and what might change.

If your entire score was a 3, you possess an awareness of the resiliency concepts and are on the way to developing a resilient organization. Continue to monitor how hardship manifests at the agency and what could help offset these issues.

If you attained a total in the 4–5 range, congratulations! Your organization is resilient. Since resiliency is not static, continue to focus attention on these vitally important concepts and their application.

> *"Resilience is our capacity to respond effectively to change, adapt to new or unforeseen conditions and circumstances, and seize an opportunity as it comes to you. It is the central characteristic of organizations that build enduring success. It is linked to sound decision-making, increased ability to process stress, and increased accountability."*
>
> "Is Your Organization Resilient?" Suzanne Smith, socialimpactarchitects.com

Suggestions to develop further organizational resiliency

- Remain responsive to changes. Allow for improvisation and be flexible to the outside world with the inevitable shifts in funding or profits, staffing, trends, and needs.
- There will always be stress in the business world. The issue is to minimize these pressures as much as possible.
- Build self-awareness with staff. It is a type of consciousness that helps everyone at the business to examine and question the realities around them. You can use mindfulness exercises that are conducive to kindness, connection, and happiness.
- Take an inventory regularly of what's working, what isn't, who are the partners, and what the organizational challenges are.
- Allow a level of risk-taking at the organization. Listen to staff for ideas on improvement and positive change.
- Reframe change to allow it to become positive. (Change is one of the few things we can count on.)

Resiliency is vital, as it gives us the will to come back from uncertain situations and helps us navigate the future in a stronger way. Resiliency can develop your strengths and allow you to apply them when you need it the most. A solution to having more organizational resiliency is to make a conscious effort to develop flexibility, adaptability, and self-awareness as a response to change.

Working in an organizational environment with consistent challenges, including having enough money, staffing needs, making a profit, and/or serving a community, can be stressful. Deliberately cultivating resiliency can help lessen anxiety while encouraging business and personal success.

Just thirty years ago, resiliency wasn't a household word or a well-known concept. Today it has become a commonplace idea. It's touted in ads for everything from glue to medicine. However, true resiliency builds the capacity to handle obstacles large and small.

It pays to consciously develop resiliency so that it's ready when needed. Fortunately, resiliency can assist us in healing individually and globally. The theme of resiliency can move humanity to a more level playing field.

> *"We are building a critical mass of future citizens who will indeed rescind the mean-spirited, greed-based, control driven social policies we now have and recreate a social covenant grounded in social and economic justice."*
>
> Bonnie Bernard, "The Foundations of the Resiliency Framework"

For-profit resiliency ideas to put into practice

- Business needs the irrepressible spirit that comes from resiliency because we can respond appropriately to challenges.
- Organizational resiliency demonstrates the importance of creating a map to recovery that can help us rebound after organizational difficulties
- Use protective factors to restore capacity to wholeness, especially after a crisis.

Nonprofit resiliency opportunities

- Work collectively on handling stress well.
- Think about how well the organization adapts after setbacks large or small. Determine the steps you will take and proceed into action.

> *"Get your organization to the place where employees feel energized by new opportunities because they have had substantial input and are a big part of making it work. Optimism is the faith that leads to achievement. Nothing can be done without hope and confidence."*
>
> Helen Keller

More research on resiliency

- "The Foundations of the Resiliency Framework," Bonnie Bernard, Resiliency in Action, https://www.resiliency.com/free-articles-resources/the-foundations-of-the-resiliency-framework/
- "How People Learn to Become Resilient," Maria Konnikova, *New Yorker*, February 11, 2016, https://www.newyorker.com/science/maria-konnikova/the-secret-formula-for-resilience
- "You Can Be a Different Person After the Pandemic," Olga Khazan, *New York Times*, https://www.nytimes.com/2021/04/06/opinion/covid-personality-change.html
- "What Makes Some People More Resilient Than Others," Eilene Zimmerman, *New York Times*, June 18, 2020, https://www.nytimes.com/2020/06/18/health/resilience-relationships-trauma.html

- "How to Remember the 5 Protective Factors That Make Your Family Strong," infographic, The Family & Youth Institute, https://www.thefyi.org/infographic-remember-5-protective-factors-make-family-strong/
- "What Is Resiliency and Why Is It So Important?" Nan Henderson, Resiliency in Action, November 2, 2012, https://www.resiliency.com/what-is-resiliency/
- "What Is Resilience?" Harold Cohen, PsychCentral.com, May 17, 2016, https://psychcentral.com/lib/what-is-resilience#1
- "Quiz: Is Your Organization Resilient?" Suzanne Smith, Social Impact Architects, on Medium, https://medium.com/@Suzanne4tx/quiz-is-your-organization-resilient-dcfc482a60b7
- "Resilience: Build Skills to Endure Hardship," Mayo Clinic Staff, https://www.mayoclinic.org/tests-procedures/resilience-training/in-depth/resilience/art-20046311

Books on resiliency

- *Resilient: How to Grow an Unmistakable Core of Calm, Strength and Happiness*, Rick Hanson and Forrest Hanson. Harmony (2020).
- *The Resiliency Handbook, Bounce Back Stronger, Smarter and with Real Self Esteem,* Nan Henderson. Resiliency in Action (2012).
- *The Resiliency Advantage: Master Change, Thrive Under Pressure, and Bounce Back from Setbacks,* Al Siebert. Berrett-Koehler Publishers (2005).

WRAPPING UP RESPECT

"Hope lies in dreams, in imagination, and in the courage of those who dare to make dreams into reality."

Jonas Salk

Humanity is experiencing a huge upheaval. With that in mind, it is time to evolve beyond what we know as traditional solutions. We can use this monumental change to transform our lives, our business, and the world as we know it. Out-of-the-box remedies are needed to address these problems.

I am offering real solutions based on experience and research for current issues facing the business world. Generally, most business needs to embrace basic values to keep up with these changes while they are pursuing profits. It can start with the essential power of respecting others. It can lead to a different kind of working together that encourages inclusion and a wisdom-based perspective.

Nonprofits require more workable and humane business strategies. Many must stop running their organizations haphazardly and hoping for the best. "Downgraded expectations," as William Clark noted, are very real for this sector.

Those running for-profit businesses need to put their money where their mouth is and realize that having a values or mission statement is only the beginning of an ongoing, lifelong process. Embracing and implementing values takes rolling up your sleeves and investing time, energy, and money. The old adage that it takes money to make money apples here.

"So much has been destroyed, I have cast my lots with those who, age after age, perversely, with no extraordinary power, reconstitute the world."

Adrienne Rich, Poet

Treating individuals as valuable and not disposable can be part of this epic shift. As John McKnight, cofounder of the ABCD Institute at Northwestern University, states:

Everyone has gifts.

Everyone has something to contribute.

Everyone cares about something, and that passion is his or her motivation to act.

The heart of this book, RESPECT, is empowerment. We need to understand that true power or empowerment doesn't seek control and take advantage of others to win. We need to create a different paradigm where equality is valued, and respect is honored. We need to start working together in a more thoughtful, compassionate way. We need to craft a community, which means inclusion of others.

We contribute our skills, talents, and abilities to positively impact others in our community. These passions and talents can be put to good use in the workforce. Participating in a business that allows us to consistently grow, change, and be appreciated for our talents is well worth doing. Together, through thoughtful choices and beginning with respect, we can create a different, more positive world.

"We are fortunate: we are alive; we are powerful; the welfare of our civilization and our species is in our hands."

Carl Sagan

Made in the USA
Middletown, DE
23 February 2022

61693853R00177